15 things to do...
...to explore
Aberdeen

Norman G Thomson

First published 2013

NGT Publishing

contact@15thingstodo.com

www.15thingstodo.com

ISBN 9780957085107

Design by Design for Business, Aberdeen

CONTENTS

INTRODUCTION

Aberdeen is truly a city of contrasts. From the history of granite, which undoubtedly shaped the architecture of the town, to the modern buildings that house many of the world's largest oil and gas exploration companies, Aberdeen has much to offer those who want to explore its past and present. From medieval times, through the wars of independence, religious unrest and the Renaissance period, Aberdeen has been at the centre of most of the events that have defined Scottish culture. Scottish the city most certainly is, but it is much more – it is a metropolitan hub in every sense. Modern bars, nightclubs, sporting venues and rock bands intersperse with the history of the city to produce a wonderful haven on the north-east coast.

Although many people believe that Old Aberdeen was where it all started, that is not actually the birthplace of the city. The first settlers arrived near to The Green, which is close to the harbour. Nonetheless, Old Aberdeen is a great place to start the exploration journey. Described as "a hidden gem in the north-east" in a guide published by Aberdeen City Council, this part of town has a medieval cathedral, a late-medieval bridge and a 15th-century college, all within a short walking distance.

St Machar's Cathedral is probably the most iconic landmark within the Old Aberdeen boundary. A fine example of a fortified kirk, with its twin towers built in the fashion of 14th-century tower houses, and walls thick enough to contain spiral staircases, the cathedral is one of the most visited places in Scotland. Standing proudly at the edge of Seaton Park, the structure, its grounds and the area where it is located depict a past that is worth taking time to appreciate.

Seaton Park links Old Aberdeen to the residential area of Bridge of Don, to the north. With its wonderful display of roses and well-kept flowerbeds, it is one of 45 parks within the city. Aberdeen is proud of its beauty and open spaces, perhaps explaining why it has been awarded the Britain in Bloom Best City category ten times since the inauguration of the award in 1963.

Hazlehead Park is the largest in Aberdeen, covering more than 400 acres. The diversity on offer is exceptional. Originally part of the Freedom Lands granted to the city in 1319, the land fell into private ownership but is now owned by the council.

Heavily wooded, Hazlehead Park is popular with walkers, naturalists and picnickers. The trails stretch for ten miles, with well-marked routes that can take up to three hours to walk. The park itself has rose gardens, a stunning collection of azaleas, rhododendrons and heather beds, and a recently renovated children's play area and pets' corner.

Although Hazlehead offers many attractions and a place to chill out on a warm summer's day, the park is probably more famous for the annual event that occurs on the third Sunday of June. For the past 50 years the Aberdeen Highland Games has attracted hundreds of thousands of visitors to the city. Locals and visitors enjoy watching athletes compete in the many events that test strength, endurance and skill, together with the spectacle of massed pipe bands and Highland dancers.

The tartan costumes of the pipers and Highland dancers are a spectacle to behold. And so too are the tartan uniforms of the city's army regiment, the Gordon Highlanders. Alexander Gordon, the 4th Duke of Gordon, raised the Gordon Highlanders in 1794. For the honour of defending king and country, Gordon sought permission from King George III to raise a regiment. As the king was in much need of military force, particularly because of the threat from Napoleon, permission was granted.

Today, the Gordon Highlanders Museum is a fascinating reminder of the regiment, from its early days serving garrison duties in Gibraltar to its final days in Basra. The exceptional collection of stories, medals, uniforms and equipment is a must-see for anyone visiting Aberdeen.

There are many other fine museums and places to visit in Aberdeen. Aberdeen Art Gallery is the largest public gallery in the north of Scotland. Attracting more than 200,000 visitors each year, the gallery houses one of the most important collections in the country, from 18th-century portraits by Raeburn to powerful 20th-century works by Paul Nash and Francis Bacon. Paintings within the granite building include excellent examples of the work of French Impressionists Monet, Renoir, Sisley and Degas, and of Post-Impressionist Toulouse-Lautrec.

The tale of granite is an important one to the aesthetics of Aberdeen. Known as the Granite City, Aberdeen owes its architectural heritage to its geological base and for many years this hard stone has been used for building. As early as the 14th century, buildings around Aberdeen were constructed, in part, with the stone. Drum Castle, built during the 1300s, and Crathes Castle, constructed in the 1500s, both have granite stone in their structures. However, it was not until much later that the demand for the material really took off.

The evolution of industry and commerce during the 18th century led to an unprecedented demand for granite. Greater horse traffic, with iron-shod cartwheels, increased the need for more durable materials for road building. Granite, because of its extremely hard properties, was ideal for this and Aberdeen began exporting the stone, particularly to London. Rubislaw Quarry, in what is now the west end of Aberdeen, became the epicentre of the granite industry in Great Britain.

The quarry, located at the Hill of Rubislaw, about two miles west of the city centre, was opened in 1740. Aberdeen City Council decided that the stone from the quarry did not have suitable potential as a building material and so gave up the rights to work the land, selling those rights to local businessmen. Since then, an estimated six million tonnes of granite have been excavated from the quarry, resulting in a man-made hole that is now 450 feet deep.

Marischal College is said to be the second-largest granite building in the world. Located on Broad Street, the building was formerly the seat of the ancient Marischal College and University of Aberdeen, which was founded in 1593.

Designed by Archibald Simpson, construction of the modern college began in 1835. Additional work was completed in 1905 by Alexander Marshall Mackenzie when he extended the property with the local stone, with the result that the building is second only to the Escorial Palace in Spain in the use of granite.

Another fine example of granite construction is evident within the Kirk of St Nicholas in the centre of Aberdeen. Originally built around 1157, the kirk was extended during the 15th and 19th centuries. After a fire in 1874, which destroyed the East Church together with the lead-clad timber tower, the church was rebuilt with a massive granite tower, which today stands prominently above the St Nicholas area of Aberdeen.

The city of Aberdeen is steeped in religious history. From the early settlers who arrived in the north-east of Scotland almost 8,000 years ago, to the battle for power during the Jacobean years, Aberdeen is a fascinating place in which to explore Scottish history.

Early hunter-gatherers first arrived in the area now known as Aberdeen around 6000BC. Establishing themselves around the mouths of the River Dee and the River Don, these early people have left little in the way of artifacts to indicate how they lived.

A more prominent reminder of lifestyle has been left by the Beaker People who inhabited Scotland around 2000BC.

Responsible for the numerous early stone circles that are abundant throughout the north-east, Beaker People were so named because of the distinctive bell-shaped pottery that has been found across the western parts of Europe, which date back as far as the third millennium BC. These people had become experts at creating a wide range of pottery receptacles.

The Romans arrived in Aberdeenshire during the first century AD. In AD84, Agricola, the Roman governor of Britannia, led a force of some 40,000 men into Caledonia, to fight armies of the then-dominant Pictish tribes. A famous battle took place outside Aberdeen, near to the hill of Bennachie, called the Battle of Mons Graupius, where it is said that local Picts took to the hills and stood their ground against the advancing troops. Ruins of a fort still stand at the summit of the 1,700-foot hill.

Bennachie is not actually a hill itself, but rather a prominent range of hills in Aberdeenshire, located about 25 miles from the centre of Aberdeen. It is one of the most popular and best-loved attractions for locals and visitors. Whether it is for spotting rare wildlife, exploring the history of the area, or simply enjoying a short trek, a walk to the top of the many peaks in the range can be invigorating and rewarding.

Wildlife can be seen much closer to the heart of the city. Aberdeen lies between two rivers, the Dee and the Don. Both rivers begin their journeys on the Cairngorm massif, at heights greater than 3,000 feet, more than 80 miles from the city. They meander majestically through some of the finest countryside in Scotland, passing through wood and farmland that are steeped in history and royal connections. But as they approach the city, their similarities of origin and of their journeys come to a dramatic end. The Dee flows into the city through the harbour, where its waters mix with those of the shipping landscape before merging into the North Sea. The Don is quite different.

The lower reaches of the River Don, and in particular the last two miles from Persley Bridge to the mouth of the river, are one of Aberdeen's hidden gems: a wildlife corridor where woodlands come right down to the banks of the water and where the river itself is home to an abundance of salmon, trout and even an otter or two. Along that two-mile stretch, woodland changes to beach where sand dunes, built up over hundreds of years, dominate the intersection of land and sea.

It is the continual interaction between the waters in the river and those of the North Sea that make the Donmouth area such a

The dunes at Donmouth

fascinating place to visit. The erosion and deposition of sand and silt by the river and sea have created and moulded an estuary that is home to an abundance of plants and animals. At low tide the mud-flats are a wading-birds' restaurant, with a variety of worms, snails and shellfish for the waders to feast upon.

The estuary at the northern end of the beach, spectacular as it is, is only one part of the beachfront. Aberdeen is a true beach city, not just a city with a beach nearby. The Esplanade, which runs for two and a half miles, is both beautiful and exciting. With a diverse range of things to do, the beachfront offers a great day out for all the family.

It takes only a ten-minute walk from the heart of the shopping district at the top end of Union Street to reach the Beach Boulevard, which is almost centrally placed along the Esplanade. From there, either side of this wide-open space presents everything for those who simply want to stroll along the wide pavements, enjoying the breeze from the North Sea, or for the more energetic who prefer rollerblading, jogging and cycling. The Esplanade definitely has something for everyone.

At the south end of the Esplanade, near to Aberdeen harbour's entrance, lies Footdee, known locally as 'fittie'. Dating back to medieval times, the first recorded reference to this area was in 1398. Footdee was once a fishing village. In 1809, in response to the demand for a purpose-built development to re-house the fishing community, John Smith, then superintendent of the town's Public Works, laid out the new 'fish town'.

Once upon a time, Aberdeen was a major fishing port. Times have changed and fishing boats have been mostly replaced with large service vessels that supply the massive oil and gas industry in the North Sea.

The influx of money and business into Aberdeen has meant that the city enjoys a certain level of affluence. New buildings have replaced some of the 1950s and 1960s structures, and modern amenities, pubs, restaurants and entertainment venues have flourished. However, even modern Aberdeen has kept its Scottish cultural roots, to offer the visitor a unique blend of past and present. Aberdeen, the Granite City, with its roots put down over 8,000 years ago, is indeed the heart of north-east Scotland.

A thriving oil capital

OLD ABERDEEN

"A hidden gem in the north-east" is how Old Aberdeen is referred to in the *Old Aberdeen Trail*, a guide to this part of the city published by Aberdeen City Council. Within the district that is now classed as Old Aberdeen it is possible to visit a medieval cathedral, a late-medieval bridge and a 15th-century college. Together with those medieval attractions, Old Aberdeen, an independent town between 1489 and 1891, offers a splendid array of 18th- and 19th-century architecture.

Standing in the heart of Old Aberdeen is one of the city's most recognisable buildings, King's College Chapel. Built from sandstone, the chapel has an impressive crown tower that was made to house the great bells used to call the faithful to mass.

The chapel at King's College, like most buildings in Old Aberdeen, was the creation of Bishop Elphinstone. Born in 1431, he graduated from Glasgow University and was ordained in 1455. He entered politics when James III included him in an embassy to the French king in 1479, and was later appointed Bishop of Aberdeen, in March 1483.

Elphinstone had a significant impact on Aberdeen, particularly Old Aberdeen. In *The Lost City* Jane Stevenson and Peter Davidson say "The most dramatic result of his overhaul of his diocese was his foundation of the University of Aberdeen. He was absolutely convinced of the need of a university for the North, and went personally to Rome to convince Pope Alexander VI that the remoteness of northern Scotland from any centre of higher learning was creating a serious shortage of lay administrators, doctors of medicine, civil lawyers, and school-masters."

The Pope confirmed his supplication in a bull of foundation dated 10 February 1495. Teaching began in October 1497, and, by 1505 when King's College received its charter, Elphinstone had collected sufficient funds to support an academic community of 36 masters and students, within five faculties.

Elphinstone died on 25 October 1514 in Edinburgh. A bronze and marble sculpture was created in his memory by Harry Wilson in the early 20th century. It sits outside King's College Chapel and

is itself remarkable in its beauty. Originally intended as a re-creation of Elphinstone's tomb, the structure was erected by Elphinstone's successor, Bishop Dunbar. The tomb is carefully described in the college inventory of 1542:

His effigy in bishop's vestments, with two angels carrying two candlesticks at the head and two beadsmen carrying the epitaph graven in brass at the feet; below, on the south side are the three theological Virtues and Contemplation; on the north side are the four cardinal Virtues distinguished by their emblems; on the east and west sides the arms of the Founder carried by angels.

Although the chapel at King's College ceased to be used for worship at the time of the Reformation, it was restored in 1891. However, the first university chaplain was not appointed until 1945. Students today attend services in the chapel and many graduates from the university hold their marriage ceremonies there. The chapel is also the heart of the university's musical life, with concerts and recitals being held regularly.

The Market Square
Further north from King's College Chapel is Market Square. When Old Aberdeen became a burgh of barony in the late 15th century it acquired the right to its own market. As such, a mercat cross had to be erected to mark the designated area for the market. The mercat cross also marked a burgh's place of public assembly, where announcements were made and punishments handed out.

The actual mercat cross of Old Aberdeen probably dates from around the middle of the 16th century. Originally highly decorated, with images of the Virgin on the north and south sides, the cross was defaced during the Reformation. It suffered further damage during the civil wars and was later sold by the council of Old Aberdeen. However, the cross has been restored and put back to its current, and original, position in the square of Old Aberdeen.

Reformation
The Reformation had a significant impact on the people of Old Aberdeen, similar to other areas of Scotland. However, the people here had more reason than those of any other burgh to view the Catholic Church with approval. Authors Stevenson and Davidson comment "Their city was a burgh of barony, for the great William Elphinstone had won them their independence from New Aberdeen. His successor, Gavin Dunbar, had endowed

a hospital, and built upon Elphinstone's beginnings with respect to their great cathedral and their university.

"The prosperity of the burgh revolved around effective, zealous and entrepreneurial Catholic bishops who were also barons. Everything the people had, everything they were proud of, came directly from the Church. Money which flowed into the Church's coffers was spent in Old Aberdeen, bringing work to craftsmen and labourers. The welling-up of genuine exasperation which fuelled the Reformation in most of Scotland was probably less felt in Old Aberdeen."

The Scottish parliament abolished papal authority throughout the realm in 1560. This meant that the celebration of mass was forbidden. A reformed ministry was established and many of the clergy who would not subscribe to the new Protestant confession were relieved of their ministry. However, unlike many areas of Scotland, Aberdeen drifted into Protestantism gradually rather than with vigour and immediacy. Although considerable damage was done to churches, Catholic clergy were not all ousted. In fact, the Menzies family, who ruled most of Aberdeen in the 16th century, bought up treasures from the parish churches and they kept on the former prior of the town's Carmelite monastery as a private chaplain.

St Machar's Cathedral in Old Aberdeen was grudgingly spared destruction during the Reformation, becoming the parish church for the district. However, the building was large, much too big for the small congregation that attended worship, and it became difficult to keep it in good order. Such was the stubbornness of the people of Old Aberdeen that it was not until around 1640, many years following the start of the Reformation, that Catholic symbols were chiselled out of the building's fabric.

Old Aberdeen develops
After the Reformation, Old Aberdeen had a population of "900 souls", according to a census of 1636. The purpose of this population survey was to identify beggars and vagabonds with the intention of expelling them from the community or compelling them to change their ways.

The largest occupation group within the burgh of Old Aberdeen was the weavers. By 1677 there were so many people selling cloth on market day that there was no room to get down the streets, so the council decided to create a designated cloth market along what is now St Machar Drive.

St Machar Drive slices Old Aberdeen into two parts: the Chanonry to the north and High Street to the south. The Chanonry derives its name from the fact that it was once home to the canons (clergy) of St Machar's Cathedral, which sits at the far end of the street. Canons probably lived in this part of Old Aberdeen from as early as 1240. Many of their manses were destroyed during the Reformation; however some plots of land where the manses once were still lie intact today.

Amidst the history of the Chanonry, with its medieval architecture, lies something of complete contrast: the Cruickshank Botanical Garden. Founded in 1898 with a bequest from Anne Cruickshank, in memory of her brother Alexander and their father who was a professor at the university, the Deed of Trust specified that the garden was to be "for the furtherance of university interests and the public good".

The Cruickshank Botanical Garden consists of a wide range of plants of interest. The Rose Garden, created in 1980, illustrates the history of rose cultivation, while the Sunken Garden, planted after the Second World War, has a fine collection of dwarf conifers and rhododendrons. There is also a wonderful Rock and Water Garden with alpines and spring bulbs.

Lady of the Snows

At the opposite end of the territory that marks Old Aberdeen, on High Street, is the Snow Kirk. Like so much else in this area of the city, the Snow Kirk owes its origins to Bishop Elphinstone. Stevenson and Davidson reflect "In the late autumn of 1494 Elphinstone began the long journey to the Pope's city, not only to present a formal report on the state of his diocese, but also with the aim of persuading Pope Alexander VI to approve his project of founding a university.

"Having entered the Vatican City through the Flaminian Gate, like all travellers from the north, he would have found it in the middle of a thorough Renaissance overhaul: St Peter's had been built in 1452 and the Sistine Chapel was under construction. However, it was one of the city churches which spoke most personally to Elphinstone, Santa Maria Maggiore (Great St Mary's), also known as St Santa Maria ad Nives [of the snows].

"The church of Santa Maria ad Nives owes its origin, so legend said, to a vision. The Virgin appeared to Pope Liberius one night in the year 352, and told him that he must build her a church on a precise area of the Esquiline Hill, which would be defined by a snowfall the following morning. Despite the sweltering heat of

walk around the
Botanical Garden and
enjoy the vibrancy
of colour

visit St Machar's Cathedral,
perhaps during an organ
recital, and reflect on
Christianity coming
to Scotland

listen to the choir
in Kings College Chapel

THE CHANONRY

walk along the
picturesque Chanonry
and enjoy some of the
original buildings of
Old Aberdeen

Highlights

an Italian August, the marvelling citizens woke to find an extensive snowfall on the Esquiline, the boundaries of which they marked out forthwith. By Elphinstone's time, it had become one of the four most important churches in Rome.

"When Old Aberdeen became a burgh of barony in 1489, its new status and dignity required it to have a parish church of its own, with bell-tower, bell, cemetery, place for holy things, baptismal font, and other things proper to a parochial church. St Mary ad Nives [of the snows] church was constructed as the parish church of Old Aberdeen.

"Elphinstone's personal devotion to Mary is indicated by his seal, with the Virgin in pride of place; by the dual dedication of the cathedral (which before the Reformation was the church of St Mary and St Machar); and by the dedication of the college, which, according to its common seal, was the college of St Mary, not King's. It was the Virgin who Elphinstone turned to 'in vigils with signs and groans', as he said in a charter of 1499, when the amount of responsibility he had taken on temporarily daunted him."

The burgh's church of Our Lady of the Snows was dedicated in 1503. Two small bells, called Schochtmadony and Skellat,

were taken from the south-west turret of St Machar's and gifted to the new foundation by the bishop and clergy of the cathedral. However, the church was only to serve the people of Old Aberdeen for less than 100 years before the Reformation. The building, although not demolished, was allowed to fall down. Today, the Snow Kirk stands reduced to the remains of its four walls, but it is still there. A secret winding path leads from the impressive Powis Gates to the grave-yard, a serene and peaceful spot that few people even know exists.

The Powis Gates were erected by John Leslie of Powis in 1833. These gates form the entrance to, confusingly, a house known as Powis Gate, now the site of two halls of residence for the university.

Memorial Garden
Finally the journey ends at the MacRobert Memorial Garden. Lady MacRobert, née Workman, was born in Worcester, Massachusetts in 1880. Daughter of a New England physician, she took a degree in geology at Imperial College, London, becoming one of the first women to be elected a fellow of the Geological Society.

In 1911, Rachel Workman married Sir Alexander MacRobert, who was born to an Aberdeen labourer and died as first baronet of Cawnpore and Cromar.

King's College Chapel

Alexander MacRobert went out to India as the managing director of the Cawnpore (Kanpur) Woollen Mill, aged 30, and became the founder of the British India Corporation, a successful textile company that is still based in Kanpur, northern India, today.

Sir Alexander died in 1922, when their eldest son was only ten. Rachel MacRobert raised her family and took over as a director of the company in India. Unfortunately, her three sons all died in aircraft accidents. The first died before the Second World War while the other two were shot down in 1941.

In October 1941, Rachel MacRobert wrote a cheque for £25,000 to the RAF for a Stirling Bomber. She wrote "I have no more sons to wear the MacRobert badge or carry it in the fight, but if I had ten sons I know they would have followed that line of duty."

Left as a wealthy widow, Lady MacRobert created the MacRobert Trust, which has given lavishly to a variety of causes over the last 50 years including the prestigious MacRobert Award, Britain's premier prize for innovation in engineering. She died at her family home in 1954.

The memorial garden was created in Old Aberdeen in 1965.

From the humble beginnings of a small market town, a burgh in its own right, to the now world-renowned University of Aberdeen, much of this area of the city is down to the vision of one man, Bishop Elphinstone. However, others have left their mark too. In fact, Old Aberdeen continually changes, if only because each new academic term brings fresh under-graduates to the city and to this unique district of Aberdeen. Whether to study or simply to cherish a journey back in time, Old Aberdeen will make a lasting impression on anyone who ventures into the area.

Inside view of the old town hall

Exploring

King's College Chapel

"The Crown Tower remains one of the most adored, historic and beautiful emblems and icons of our university," says the website of the University of Aberdeen. The chapel is open to visitors Monday to Friday from 10am to 3.30pm.

Information about King's College can be found on the university website.
www.abdn.ac.uk/chaplaincy/chapel

Worship at King's College Chapel

Serving as a constant reminder of the university's foundations, the chapel brings together the past, present and future for the people of Old Aberdeen and for visitors to the area. Worship is held each Sunday during term-time, with an evening Mass also conducted. The Chapel Choir uplifts every Sunday service with beautiful and professional praise.
www.abdn.ac.uk/about/worship

The Aberdeen Bestiary

One of the earliest treasures of the university's collection, which has been conserved at King's College, is a manuscript that was written around the year 1200. Known as the Aberdeen Bestiary, the document attempts an account of all God's works in nature. This "book of the visible world" includes animals and birds, fishes, plants, monsters and imaginary beings. The manuscript used to reside in the old

Royal Library at Westminster Palace. It still bears its Westminster shelf-mark (number 158) and is recognisable in the shelf list made in 1542. It is thought that the manuscript was presented to Thomas Reid, regent of Marischal College and Latin secretary to James VI early in the 17th century, possibly as a retirement gift.

Information about the Bestiary can be found on the university website.
www.abdn.ac.uk/bestiary

The Sibyls

Among the treasures and curiosities of Old Aberdeen is a set of ten paintings, survivors of a set of 12, of the Sibyls: legendary women of the ancient world who were believed in Christian tradition to have experienced prophetic visions of aspects of the life of Christ.

Commissioned by William Guild, principal of King's College from 1640 to 1651, the paintings were shown in the old Common Hall of the college. They represent one of the very first commissions of art in Scotland.

These paintings are located in King's College.

The Old Town House

The University of Aberdeen has recently restored the Old Town House as part of its commitment to conserving historic buildings of Old Aberdeen.

With the open market directly outside, the Old Town House would have been a hub of activity for this area. Tolls would have been collected, criminals imprisoned and meetings of the council would have been held. The building was paid for by subscriptions from the local merchants' society, the Incorporated Trades and the Masonic Lodge, who all had rights to use the building for meetings.

The Old Town House is located right in the heart of Old Aberdeen. In the reception area there is a wealth of information on Old Aberdeen including trail guides to help the visitor to discover the history and culture of this area of the city.
www.abdn.ac.uk/oldtownhouse

Cruickshank Botanical Garden

Founded in 1898 with a bequest from Anne Cruickshank in memory of her brother and their father, the garden is open to the public. Opening times can be found on the university website.
www.abdn.ac.uk/botanic-garden

St Machar's Cathedral

The cathedral is a fine example of a fortified kirk. The twin towers are built in the fashion of 14th-century tower houses, with walls thick enough to contain spiral staircases to the upper floors, and battlements at the tower heads. Between the towers on the west side there are seven narrow windows. In the ruined transepts on the east side, on sandstone columns, there are carved features: a merman, mermaid and leaves. Craftsmen drew on fantasy as well as nature to the glory of God. Inside the cathedral, on the south side, the St Machar window, by Douglas Strachan, an Aberdeen artist, tells the traditional story of the founding of the first church in the 6th century.

If you have a few hours to spare, St Machar's is a great place to visit. There is the cathedral itself, but the grounds are also worth a look.

The cathedral, which is open daily to visitors, is located on the Chanonry, off St Machar Drive in Old Aberdeen.
www.stmachar.com

Seaton Park

St Machar's Cathedral stands overlooking Seaton Park which marks the end of Old Aberdeen. There is an entrance to the park, which sits adjacent to the River Don, near the main gates of the cathedral.

Old Aberdeen Trail

Aberdeen City Council has published an excellent guide to Old Aberdeen, the Old Aberdeen Trail. On this walk, which should take two to three hours, the main features of this part of Aberdeen can be found, together with a number of commemorative plaques, carved stones and armorial panels.

Detail of the guide can be found on the Aberdeen City Council website.
www.aberdeencity.gov.uk

DONMOUTH LOCAL NATURE RESERVE AND BEYOND

The city of Aberdeen lies between two rivers, the Dee and the Don. Both rivers begin their journeys on the Cairngorm massif, at heights greater than 3,000 feet, more than 80 miles from the city. They meander majestically through some of the finest countryside in Scotland, passing through wood and farmland that are steeped in history and royal connections. But as they approach the city, their similarities of origin and of their journeys come to a dramatic end. The Dee flows into the city through the harbour, where its waters mix with those of the shipping landscape before emerging into the North Sea. The Don is quite different.

The lower reaches of the River Don, and in particular the last two miles from Persley Bridge to the mouth of the river, are one of Aberdeen's hidden gems: a wildlife corridor where woodlands come right down to the banks of the water and where the river itself is home to an abundance of salmon, trout and even an otter or two. Along that two-mile stretch, woodland changes to beach where sand dunes, built up over hundreds of years, dominate the intersection of land and sea.

It is the continual interaction between the waters in the river and those of the North Sea that make the Donmouth area such a fascinating place to visit. The erosion and deposition of sand and silt by the river and sea have created and moulded an estuary that is home to an abundance of plants and animals. At low tide the mudflats are a wading-birds' restaurant, with a variety of worms, snails, and shellfish for the waders to feast upon.

Ian Talboys, an officer from the Countryside Ranger Service, comments "Donmouth is a good place to see a wide range of birds. In the summer, look out for common and sandwich terns along with the larger gannets diving from the air for fish.

"As the tide falls and more of the mudflats are exposed, many species of wading birds will move in to feed. These will include redshanks with their long red legs, and black and white oystercatchers with their carrot-like orange beaks.

"Sanderlings will rush around the water's edge like wind-up toys, while seaweed turnstones will live up to their name and turn over stones and weeds in the hunt for insects and crabs.

"Many birds migrate to this area during the winter months, particularly from Northern Europe and Scandinavia, while others come to us for the summer months. Common terns will often be seen flying acrobatically along the river, diving from 20 feet into the water to catch a fish. Sometimes we get visits from warblers that have been blown off-track from their migratory routes through Eastern Europe. It is a very interesting place."

Diversity of wildlife

Dominating this area of the nature reserve are the sand dunes that line the estuary and the grasses that are able to flourish in this mobile system. Few plant species are able to cope with the constantly shifting sand. Marram grass and sea lyme grass are two species that have been able to adapt to being buried by sand and to the lack of moisture. The latter species is not native to the area, and it is thought that it may have been introduced unintentionally early in the 1800s, perhaps by fishing boats. For many years this species remained uncommon but from about 1870 onwards it spread rapidly along the banks of the estuary.

Designated a Local Nature Reserve in 1992, there is much more to Donmouth than the estuary. From the sand dunes and mudflats up to the Brig o' Balgownie

the landscape and wildlife of the nature reserve change dramatically. "In the woodland along the river listen for all the different birds," says Ian. "Great tits sound like a creaking door hinge, chiffchaffs say their own name, while the garden warbler has a distinctive fluty call.

"Willow warblers, blackcaps and white-throats feed on the masses of insects on the trees. Overhead, swallows, swifts and house martins feed on midges flying over the river.

"Grey seals often haul themselves onto the muddy edges of the island just up-stream from the bridge over King Street. In the evening, roe deer and foxes can often be seen in the dense woodland."

Although some older oak and elm trees are present, most of the woodland was planted in the 1930s. Sycamore, ash, beech and alder line the steep slopes of the riverbank while tufted hair-grass, red campion, wild garlic and lady fern provide ground cover. Sweet cicely fills the air with the scent of aniseed during July and August, while the coconut fragrance of the gorse is present in June.

Although the slopes lining the river are quite steep, particularly on the south side, there are numerous gaps in the

Common tern

woodland where it is possible to get right down to the river's edge. About 50 feet east of the ancient Brig o' Balgownie, on the south side of the river, is one such place to enjoy the gentle lapping of the water. Mallard ducks spend most of their time on the water and can be enjoyed from this vantage point. In spring, it is usual to see females with a raft of a dozen or more fluffy ducklings following on behind.

Right on the western boundary of the Donmouth Local Nature Reserve is the old Brig o' Balgownie, which is now classified as a Scheduled Ancient Monument. Built in the 13th century, and renovated in 1605, the bridge is constructed of granite and sandstone. Spanning over 40 feet, with an apex at 50 feet above the waterline, the bridge provided access for armies to march along the eastern coast of Aberdeenshire. It also provided an important route into the city.

The bridge today is not open to cars. Instead, pedestrians and cyclists can enjoy the wonderful view from the top. Downstream, looking eastwards towards the sea, there is the Donmouth Estuary, while westwards the fast-flowing waters emerge from Seaton Park, calmed by the deep pool known as Black Neuk, directly under the bridge.

Beyond the nature reserve

Seaton Park is outwith the boundaries of the Donmouth Local Nature Reserve but is easily accessible by taking a short walk through the Cottown of Balgownie, a collection of picturesque cottages near to the bridge. Seaton Park is formed on the central part of what was once the Seaton estate. Little is known about the early history of the estate; however the name may mean 'farm town by the sea'.

Seaton House, built in the 18th century, was constructed from brick, not stone as was usual for Scottish houses. The house burnt to the ground in 1963 and today a fountain marks its approximate location.

There are many fine areas in Seaton Park. The Cathedral Walk, which leads past stunning rose beds up to St Machar's Cathedral, is always resplendent during the summer months, and a firm favourite with visitors to Aberdeen.

Continuing westwards from the Donmouth Local Nature Reserve and Seaton Park, the banks of the River Don are steeped in the history of industrial evolution, offering an excellent opportunity to explore a crucial part of Aberdeen's past, and present.

To visit this area one must first exit Seaton Park near to Benholm's Lodge, a fortified townhouse built in the 16th

Grey seal

century by Sir Robert Keith of Benholm. The exit at the lodge leads onto Tillydrone Road and, taking a right turn, with the river on the right-hand side, Tillydrone Road leads onto Gordon's Mills Road.

"The history of Gordon's Mill, on the banks of the River Don, can be traced back to the 16th century," says Chris Croly, historian with Aberdeen City Council. "There has been a mill on the site since at least the middle of the century, when the Bishop of Aberdeen, William Gordon, granted a charter 'astricting the Crofts and rigs of Old Aberdeen, as well as the lands of Cotton, and thirling them to the Mill of Gordonsmilne'. This initial charter established a very long and successful association with industry on the river.

"Starting as a small corn-milling site on a bend on the south bank of the river, the area developed into an industrial estate during the industrial revolution. By the beginning of the 20th century, the site was dominated by the Don Paper Works, a major employer for the local population."

Grandholm
Continuing west along Gordon's Mills Road, the road leads down a cobbled street towards Grandholm Bridge. Built to allow access for employees coming

to the industrial site from Woodside, a developing area in its own right, the bridge across the river provided access to another important industrial site on the river's bank.

The first charter with regard to the area of Grandholm, pronounced Grannum, was issued by Robert the Bruce, probably in the 14th century. The land changed hands several times until, on 12 January 1459, John Bannerman resigned the lands to the baillies and councillors of Aberdeen, becoming the Freedom Lands of the city of Aberdeen. The Freedom Lands were all feued (allocated for rent) by the burgh in 1551, beginning a long association with industry in this area of the city.

Chris Croly comments "The first mill at Grandholm was established by Leys, Still and Company in 1792. This company entered into an agreement with John Paton of Grandholm to cut a canal, as they called it, from the River Don to their site here to bring a new source of water power to their mill. The work of cutting this channel, which was in excess of a mile long, took several hundred workers more than two years to complete.

"Several thousand people, probably from the nearby Woodside area of the city, found work at the mill. To help the local

Brig o' Balgownie, now a Scheduled Ancient Monument

population cross the river to the factory the company built a bridge, now known as the Grandholm Bridge. However, the use of the bridge and Jacob's Ladder, a steep stairway of 66 steps down the riverbank, meant a walk of a quarter of a mile to reach the works gate. So, in 1922 a new bridge was built near the entrance to the factory, with a concrete stairway of 97 steps leading up to Gordon's Mills Road.

"Unfortunately, the firm went bankrupt in 1848. However, the site was acquired in 1859 by the firm J & J Crombie, which led to a period of great expansion. In 1851 the company purchased a large water wheel, which was 24 feet in diameter and it was recorded that '30 horses were required to move the wheel across Grandholm Bridge'.

"Crombie expanded into lucrative foreign markets. During the American Civil War, Crombie produced the Confederate Army's famous Rebel Grey cloth. This was because most mills in America were in New England, and under no circumstances would the confederates buy cloth from the Yankee states."

By the 1920s Crombie had over 320 looms on the site, employing over 1,000 people. However, as the older generation of Crombies died, there were no young ones to replace them. The company was sold in 1923 to the Salts of Saltaire, West Yorkshire.

New fashions in management started to emerge, with the introduction of time and motion studies, industrial psychology and efficiency programmes. The firm embraced these new trends, preparing them for the onslaught of the Second World War.

Suffering only minimal damage during air raids on the city, the mill went from strength to strength. Government contracts for uniforms and coats brought work to the mill and, although profits were low, the work ensured that employment in the area was maintained throughout the war years.

Continuing to trade under the Crombie name, by 1950 the mill became Britain's fourth-largest exporter of cloth to America and the largest producer of tweed in the United Kingdom. However, after many generations of local families working for the mill, the company closed the site in the 1990s.

Chris Croly says "The firm had seen many ups and downs during its life on the banks of the River Don. It is a great example of a company that grew through the industrial revolution, employing

stop by the
Workers Memorial in
the walled garden near
to Persley Bridge

stroll over
the centuries-old
bridge and marvel
at Cottown
of Balgownie

walk along the
riverbank and explore
the old machinery

watch the ducks
as they dive for
food near to
the old bridge

Highlights

41

generation after generation of local workers. It has been an integral part of the fabric and social and economic life of the area."

Grandholm is now a housing development, but it is still possible to see the channels that were cut to divert water from the fast-flowing river. All along both sides of the river, relics from the industrial past can be seen, including the cogs and wheels of the machinery that opened and closed the lades used to power the mills.

A mile inland from Grandholm is Persley Bridge, one of the major crossing points over the River Don. An important reminder of the history of Aberdeen is located at the south-west corner of the bridge, March Stone 49.

Croly comments "The march stones define an area that was known as the Freedom Lands. In 1313, Robert the Bruce granted Aberdeen custodianship of his hunting grounds. Aberdeen went on to purchase further land but, in 1551, for financial reasons, Aberdeen applied to Mary Queen of Scots for the rights to let these lands. This meant that in return for a yearly payment, lands became privately managed.

"The earliest boundary markers were probably natural features such as burns or stones. The first description of the marches dates back to a 'riding of the marches' in 1525. The practice of riding the boundary lines was intended to ensure they were being observed and respected, and that no adjacent landowners had encroached onto the town's lands."

A new system of marking the boundary of the town's lands was introduced in the 1700s. Croly continues "This style, which is still with us today, has a number coupled with the letters ABD for Aberdeen and in the case of the inner march stones the additional letters CR for either City Royalty or City Regality. The entire marking system was completed in 1810."

As one admires the view of the fast-flowing River Don from the Persley Bridge, it may be difficult to appreciate the complexity of the history, and its impact on the culture, of this area of Aberdeen. If the history associated with the industrial evolution of the area were not interesting enough, the final two miles of the river's journey from the Cairngorm mountains to the North Sea have an abundance of wildlife to be enjoyed. This relatively small area of Aberdeen is a must-see.

March stone

Exploring

Donmouth

The Donmouth Local Nature Reserve is two miles north of the centre of Aberdeen on King Street. There is plenty of roadside parking on the Esplanade, which is off King Street on the right at the Bridge of Don.

The Brig o' Balgownie is located off Balgownie Road, at the end of the road marked Cottown of Balgownie, where there is a small car-parking area.

The best way to explore the Donmouth is to walk a circuit from the Esplanade up to the Brig o' Balgownie, cross the brig and return on the other side of the river. If visiting by car, park on the Esplanade, about 100 feet from the Bridge of Don. After enjoying the estuary, the beach and mudflats, walk towards the bridge. Cross King Street at the lights and take the footpath on the left bank of the river. Watch out for seals that may be visiting the little island just past the Bridge of Don.

About 50 feet before the Brig o' Balgownie, stop to enjoy the ducks that inhabit this part of the river. Watch out for the common golden eye male, a medium-sized sea duck, with its greenish-gloss head and circular white patch below the eye. Goosanders can be seen in large numbers and so too can tufted ducks.

Before crossing the Brig o' Balgownie, take a few moments to enjoy the cobbled streets of Cottown of Balgownie. On the other side of the brig, walk back along the north bank of the river, back to the beach area of Donmouth.

At a leisurely pace, the circuit around the Donmouth Local Nature Reserve will take about two hours to complete.

During the summer months Countryside Officers from the ranger service organise many public events at Donmouth. Activities such as bird watching, sea-shore searches and mini-beast hunts are popular. "Even if people are not particularly interested in bird watching or insects, simply getting out into the fresh air for an afternoon's walk can be exciting and fun in this area," says Ian Talboys of the City Council Countryside Ranger Service. "All this fantastic biodiversity is there waiting to be explored, so get out there and see what you can find."

The Aberdeen City Council website contains maps and information about the area. **www.aberdeencity.gov.uk**

Seaton Park

The park can be accessed from the cobbled streets of Cottown of Balgownie. There is a small entry point on the right, about 70 feet from the Brig o' Balgownie. A short walk along a footpath, with the river on the right, will lead into the main park.

Alternatively, the main entrance to the park can be accessed from Seaton Place, off King Street.

Grandholm

Grandholm Village, once the site of the Crombie mills, can be accessed from Gordon's Mills Road, via the Grandholm Bridge. Although the bridge is closed to vehicular traffic it provides pedestrian access across the river to Grandholm Village. The village is now a housing development but some of the original lades and river channels can be seen.

With about two hours to spare, it is possible to walk along the riverbank from Grandholm to the Persley Bridge. After crossing the Grandholm Bridge, head along the straight road that leads from the bridge until it turns sharply to the right. Instead of turning right, go left onto Grandholm Drive, a narrow cobbled road. Shortly, this road will lead to a footpath along the banks of the river. Great examples of the machinery that were once used to open and close the water gates are still present today. This path leads to the Persley Bridge, where it is possible to see March Stone 49, at the south-west corner of the bridge. Walk back along the other bank of the river, back to the Grandholm Bridge.

Care should be taken while walking along the riverbank, particularly during wet conditions. The bank can become quite slippery and the fast-moving water can often make it hazardous.

RELIGION AND REBELLION

The city of Aberdeen is steeped in religious history. From the early settlers who arrived in the north-east of Scotland almost 8,000 years ago, to the battle for power during the Jacobean years, Aberdeen is a fascinating place in which to explore Scottish history.

Early hunter-gatherers first arrived in the area now known as Aberdeen around 6000BC. Establishing themselves around the mouths of the River Dee and the River Don, these early people have left little in the way of artifacts to indicate how they lived.

A more prominent reminder of lifestyle has been left by the Beaker People who inhabited Scotland around 2000BC. Responsible for the numerous early stone circles that are abundant throughout the north-east, Beaker People were so named because of the distinctive bell-shaped pottery that has been found across the western parts of Europe and date back as far as the third millennium BC. These people had become experts at creating a wide range of pottery receptacles.

The Romans arrived in Aberdeenshire during the first century AD. In AD84, Agricola, the Roman governor of

Britannia, led a force of some 40,000 men into Caledonia, to fight armies of the then-dominant Pictish tribes. A famous battle took place outside Aberdeen, near to the hill of Bennachie, called the Battle of Mons Graupius, where it is said that local Picts took to the hills and stood their ground against the advancing troops. Ruins of a fort still stand at the summit of the 1,700-foot hill.

The origins of the Picts in Scotland are clouded with many fables, legends and fabrications. There are many theories as to who they were, where they came from, how they lived, and whether they had spiritual beliefs. Even the monumental Pictish stones that are abundant in this area have baffled scientists and anthropologists for many years. However, one legend that has stood the test of time and is of utmost importance in the religious history of Aberdeen, is that of St Machar.

St Machar's Cathedral
Karen Ferguson, religious historian in Aberdeen, says "St Machar is said to have been a companion of Columba, who had a quest to evangelise the Picts in Scotland. Columba was born in Ireland, in modern County Donegal, part of the provinces of Ulster in the north of Ireland.

"Columba travelled to Scotland in 563 where, according to legend, he first landed on the Kintyre Peninsula. Because he could still see his native land across the water, he moved further north, up the west coast of Scotland. He was granted land on the island of Iona, where he established his religious centre.

"Columba's reputation as a holy man led to his role as diplomat among the tribes. There are many stories of miracles that he performed during his work to convert the Picts to Christianity. He visited pagan kings in what is now Inverness and formed many churches in the Hebrides. He turned his monastery at Iona into a school for missionaries.

"The link to Aberdeen comes via one of Columba's companions, St Machar. Legend has it that St Machar was told by either Columba, or God, to find a place where a river bends into the shape of a bishop's crosier, before it flows into the sea. The River Don bends in just this way where St Machar's Cathedral now stands. It is thought that St Machar formed the first site of worship where the cathedral is now located."

This early place of worship became a cathedral in the 1130s, when the seat of the bishop was transferred from Aberdeenshire to Old Aberdeen under instruction from King David I (1124–53),

regarded as one of the most significant rulers in Scotland's history. The Davidian Revolution is a term used to summarise the changes that took place during his reign. These included the formation of burghs, the creation of monasteries, and the Normanisation of the Scottish government. By 1165, a Norman-style cathedral stood on the site of St Machar's early place of worship.

During the 13th century, St Machar's Cathedral underwent extensive restoration. Started under the instruction of the Bishop of Cheyne (1282–1328), work was interrupted by the Scottish Wars of Independence.

Wars of Independence

Karen Ferguson comments "The first war began with the English invasion of Scotland in 1296. King Edward I invaded Scotland, fighting the first battle at Berwick. Edward removed the Stone of Destiny from Scone Abbey and took it to Westminster Abbey, resulting in a subduing of the Scottish people. Originally, the stone was thought to have been taken to Scotland around 330BC by the first king of Scots, Fergus, who came across the water from Ireland.

"Edward captured the stone as 'spoils of war' and had it transported to London where it was fitted into a wooden chair, known as King Edward's Chair. Most

monarchs since then have been crowned on the chair. In 1996, in a symbolic response to the growing dissatisfaction among Scots, the British government decided to return the stone to Scotland. On 15 November of that year, after a handover ceremony at the Border, the stone was transported to Edinburgh Castle where it resides today. An agreement has been made that the Scots will loan the stone whenever it is needed for the coronation of a new monarch.

"A year after the invasion by King Edward, revolts broke out, led by William Wallace. Little is known of Wallace's early years, but such was the impact of his leadership that Edward was forced to send more soldiers to deal with the Scots. Although Wallace and his men lost many battles, eventually the first major victory occurred at Stirling Bridge. Wallace was appointed Guardian of Scotland in March 1298.

"Wallace evaded capture by the English until August 1305, when he was turned over to English soldiers by the Scottish knight, John de Menteith, who was loyal to King Edward. Wallace was tried for treason. He was hanged, beheaded, and his body cut into four parts. Legend has it that his left arm was interred within the walls of St Machar's Cathedral in Aberdeen."

The armies of King Edward ravaged much of the north-east of Scotland, including Aberdeen. St Machar's Cathedral was ransacked during this time. Bishop Alexander Kinimund II demolished the cathedral in the late 14th century, because of its poor condition after the onslaught by Edward's men, and began rebuilding the nave, including the granite columns and towers at the western end.

Later bishops continued the building work, adding a central tower, the roof and paving stones. In 1520 a ceiling of panelled oak was commissioned by Bishop Gavin Dunbar. The ceiling contains 48 heraldic shields in three rows of 16. At the east end of the ceiling are the principals of each group. In the centre, Pope Leo X is followed by the Scottish archbishops and bishops in order of importance.

Over the proceeding years, about 30 canons would have performed religious and practical duties at the cathedral. St Machar's had an important role in the political and spiritual development of the north-east of Scotland. However, change once again loomed.

In 1560, the Parliament of Scotland enacted the Papal Jurisdiction Act, declaring that the Pope had no jurisdiction in Scotland. The church was re-established along reformed lines, with Protestantism and Presbyterianism as the predominant faith. St Machar's lost its status as a cathedral; its treasures were taken away and most of its land sold.

The church in Scotland was to be at the centre of more troubles when Oliver Cromwell, an English military and political leader, temporarily overthrew the monarchy in England. After having King Charles I executed, Cromwell invaded Scotland. He made a famous appeal to the Church of Scotland, urging them to see the error of their royal alliance – the Scots had proclaimed Charles II, son of Charles I, as king. Cromwell conquered Scotland and ruled as Lord Protector from 1653 until his death in 1658.

Cromwell's men, under George Monck, ransacked Dundee, killing up to 2,000 people and destroying 60 ships in the harbour. He led his troops into Aberdeen, looking for material to build his fort on Castlehill which overlooked the harbour (a bastion still remains today). Some of the material came from the Bishop of St Machar's palace, and from part of the cathedral. It is not clear whether the destruction of some of the cathedral led to weakening of the base of the central tower, but in 1688 a storm caused its fall into the transepts.

The Glorious Revolution

Several years later, the Glorious Revolution occurred. William of Orange, a Dutch ruler, overthrew King James VII of Scotland and II of England. William's successful invasion of England with a Dutch fleet and army led to him ascending the throne, as William III, jointly with his wife, Mary.

The main reason for William of Orange getting involved with English and Scottish politics was that the political circles in this country were troubled by King James' policies of religious tolerance, his Catholicism and his close ties with France. In 1688, James had a son by his second wife, the Roman Catholic Mary of Modena. The wars over religion were fresh in the minds of the population and many people feared a revived Catholic dominance of the government if the son of James II became king (James had two earlier daughters from his first marriage, both being raised as Protestants and the elder being the true heir to the throne). Suspecting that the son would become the next monarch, and worried about the repercussions of a return to Catholicism, key leaders of the government invited William of Orange to England. William indicated that military intervention would be needed.

Following his defeat, James II fled to France. William of Orange threatened to withdraw his troops from England and Scotland, and so convinced the government to make himself and his wife joint monarchs. Mary was actually the eldest daughter of James II by his first wife, and was a Protestant.

This revolution permanently ended any chance of Catholicism returning to the throne of England, its effects being disastrous both socially and politically. Catholics were denied the right to vote and the monarch was forbidden to be, or to marry, a Catholic.

Jacobites

James II had cultivated support on the fringes of his kingdoms, however, particularly in the Highlands of Scotland. Supporters of James, known as Jacobites, were prepared to resist what they saw as an illegal coup by force of arms. The first Jacobite rebellion took place in 1689.

Another event that aggravated the situation was the Act of Union in 1707. The Union with Scotland Act was passed in 1706 by the Parliament of England, while the Union with England Act, passed in 1707 by the Parliament of Scotland, sealed the union of the kingdoms into a single country, Great Britain, with a single monarch and a single parliament, based in Westminster, London.

This union fuelled the Jacobites, pushing them away from the legitimate political process. Furthermore, after the death of William of Orange, Anne, the daughter of James II, became queen. However, she died without a living heir and the monarchy passed to the next claimant, George I.

George was born in Hanover, in what is now Germany. After the death of Queen Anne, George ascended the British throne as the first monarch of the House of Hanover. Although over 50 Roman Catholics bore closer blood relationships to Anne, Catholics were prohibited from inheriting the throne. George was the closest living Protestant relative.

In reaction, the Jacobites attempted to depose George and replace him with Anne's Catholic half-brother, James Francis Edward Stuart, but their attempts failed.

Karen comments "Aberdeen had an important part to play in the Jacobite rebellions. There was definite anti-Hanoverian feeling in the city, strong enough for a rebel Jacobite council to be elected. The council set about raising taxes to help their cause.

"An important landmark during the Jacobite years, which is still in the city today, is the Mercat Cross. Dating

Robert the Bruce statue at Marischal College

reflect on the suffering
during the Jacobean wars
at the Tolbooth Museum

explore the rich history
and heritage of the
Kirk of St Nicholas,
right in the centre
of the city

relax near to the
Mercat Cross and
remember all those
kings and queens
who shaped the culture
of Aberdeen

visit
St Machar's Cathedral,
the seat of religion
in the city

Highlights

from 1686, the cross was used for the proclamation of new monarchs. The symbolism in making such announcements was important to the rebels and, on 20 September 1715, James Francis Edward Stuart, the Jacobite 'pretender to the throne of Great Britain', was declared king.

"The day following the declaration of the new king, the rebels held elections for a new council. Those loyal to the Hanoverians abstained from the meeting, while the Jacobite councillors met in the East Kirk of St Nicholas.

"However, the rebels lacked military leadership, and their armies failed to act as a cohesive force, soon to become over-powered by English armies.

"The second Jacobite rebellion took place during 1745, led by Prince Charles Edward Stuart, son of James Francis Edward Stuart. Charles, better known as Bonnie Prince Charlie, landed on the west coast of Scotland in July 1745, accompanied by only nine men and few arms. The uprising suffered from poor timing, bad organisation and false hope. With few successes under his belt, Charlie marched south in an attempt to recruit English followers. However, only 200 men joined his army. Charles had to retreat back to Scotland and was finally halted at the Battle of Culloden by the Duke of Cumberland. He escaped from the battle-field and lurked in the western isles under the care of Flora MacDonald, who escorted the prince 'over the sea to Skye'.

"An army, led by the Duke of Cumberland, entered Aberdeen in 1746 and restored order within the council and city. He arrived with five regiments of dragoons and 16 regiments of foot soldiers. Some of his troops were quartered at what was then the newly built Robert Gordon's Hospital. The troops made several alterations to the building, including bricking up windows and digging a defensive ditch around the structure.

"During groundwork for an extension to the college in 2000, archeologists uncovered a portion of ditch which they were able to excavate. Finds in the ditch, which included fragments of bowls, stems of clay pipes, and fragments of beer bottles, were dated to the 18th century. It is believed that those were used by Cumberland's men before they marched off to Culloden.

"The Tolbooth, built between 1616 and 1629, had a significant role to play after the rebellion. Known and suspected Jacobites were taken to the Tolbooth to await trial. A list of prisoners taken into the building is held by Aberdeen City

Archives and records show that 96 prisoners, many of whom were craftsmen or servants, were taken 'in the Tolbooth for treasonable practices …'

"The Tolbooth is now Aberdeen's Museum of Civic History. One of the cells, known as the Jacobite cell, explores this part of the city's history. An interactive model of Willie Baird, a real prisoner from 1746, sits next to his Jacobite compatriots, James Innes and Alexander Annand, as they await their trial."

From the days of Columba, when St Machar, one of his companions, first established a place of worship in the city, to the romantic characters of the Jacobite years, Aberdeen is steeped in the history of religion and rebellion. Aberdeen has been at the centre of the cultural evolution of Scotland, making it a fascinating place to explore the essence of past and present.

Exploring

St Machar's Cathedral

The cathedral is a fine example of a fortified kirk. The twin towers are built in the fashion of 14th-century tower houses, with walls thick enough to contain spiral staircases to the upper floors, and battlements at the tower heads. Between the towers on the west side there are seven narrow windows. In the ruined transepts on the east side, on sandstone columns, there are carved features: a merman, mermaid and leaves. Craftsmen drew on fantasy as well as nature to the glory of God. Inside the cathedral, on the south side, the St Machar window, by Aberdeen artist Douglas Strachan, tells the traditional story of the founding of the first church in the 6th century.

If you have a few hours to spare, St Machar's is a great place to visit. There is the cathedral itself, but the grounds are also worth a look.

The cathedral, which is open daily to visitors, is located on The Chanonry, off St Machar Drive in Old Aberdeen.
www.stmachar.com

The Tolbooth Museum

The Tolbooth Museum is one of Aberdeen's oldest buildings and one of the best-preserved gaols in Scotland. Within the museum there are displays on local history and on the development of crime and punishment.

The Tolbooth houses the former wardhouse, or prison, a complex of 17th- and 18th-century gaol cells. The unique atmosphere within the cells provides a striking experience and a real insight into imprisonment and treatment of prisoners during the Jacobite years.

Open daily, except Mondays, the Tolbooth Museum is located off Union Street, near to the King Street Junction.
www.aagm.co.uk

The Mercat Cross

Located in the Castlegate, the Aberdeen Mercat Cross was built in 1686 by John Montgomery, a local mason, reputedly at a cost of £100. This fine structure comprises a large hexagonal base for the vertical post, which is topped with a white unicorn. The base is highly decorated, including medallions with illustrations of ten of the Stuart monarchs.

The Kirk of St Nicholas

The Kirk of St Nicholas has been at the heart of Aberdeen, providing spiritual worship since its ancient establishment in the 12th century. It is arguably the most important building in the royal burgh of Aberdeen. The present structure is mainly of the 18th and 19th centuries, but it incorporates portions from the 12th century.

The kirk and kirkyard have been used for burial for at least 900 years. Several fine monuments of the 17th century, and later, survive within the grounds of the kirk.

Visitors are welcome at the Kirk of St Nicholas, which is located in the city centre of Aberdeen. From May to September, the kirk is open daily. There are volunteers on site during opening times to answer any questions or to show people around. There are daily prayers at 1pm, held in the Cowan Chapel in the West Kirk.
www.kirk-of-st-nicholas.org.uk

Artifacts of the Jacobite Period

Aberdeen City Council's numismatic collection contains more than 100 coins of the first two Hanoverian kings of Great Britain, George I and George II. These coins would have been in circulation at the time of the Jacobite rebellions.

There are two propaganda medals, which bear the Latin word *Reddite*, meaning 'restore (my Kingdom to me)'.

Aberdeen Art Gallery and Museums Collections contain a flintlock pistol, said to have been used at the Battle of Culloden.
www.aagm.co.uk
www.aberdeencity.gov.uk

61

ABERDEEN'S COASTAL PATH

THE ESPLANADE

Aberdeen is a true beach city, not just a city with a beach nearby. The Esplanade, which runs for two and a half miles, is both beautiful and exciting. With a diverse range of things to do on it, the beachfront offers a great day out for all the family.

It takes only a ten-minute walk from the heart of the shopping district at the top end of Union Street to reach the Beach Boulevard, which is almost centrally placed along the Esplanade. From there, either side of this wide-open space presents everything for those who simply want to stroll along the wide pavements, enjoying the breeze from the North Sea, or for the more energetic who prefer rollerblading, jogging and cycling. The Esplanade definitely has something for everyone.

At the south end of the Esplanade, near to Aberdeen harbour's entrance, lies Footdee, known locally as 'fittie'. Dating back to medieval times, the first recorded reference to this area was in 1398. Footdee was once a fishing village. In 1809, in response to the demand for a purpose-built development to re-house the fishing community, John Smith, then superintendent of the town's Public Works, laid out the new 'fish town'.

The two regimented squares of Footdee originally contained 28 single-storey thatched houses. The number of houses was increased in 1837 and 1855 when Middle Row and Pilot Square, respectively, were added to the town. The architect William Smith, son of John and the designer of Balmoral Castle, added further houses, and constructed additional storeys to some of the existing dwellings. This much-needed space allowed more families to move into the harbour area, at a time when fishing had become one of the main industries in the town.

During the late 19th century the town council sold the dwellings to occupiers, resulting in a period of great development in the area. Individual expression was now the norm, with each house becoming slightly different and unique. Tarry sheds, originally constructed from driftwood and other found materials, were added to the communal land, adding character to the place. Although most of the sheds have been rebuilt, some of the original constructions remain today. The entire village of Fittie was given Conservation Area status in 1968.

Footdee owes its existence to the importance of the harbour. The sheltered estuary of the River Dee, where it meets the North Sea, attracted settlers from Holland and the Rhineland as long ago as 2000BC. But it was not until the developments during the middle of the 1800s that the long-term future of Aberdeen harbour was to be secured.

Aberdeen Harbour

In 1136, King David I of Scotland granted the Bishops of Aberdeen the right to levy a fee on all ships trading at the port. Increasing links with Europe resulted in the harbour growing in popularity with the owners of merchant vessels, and hence income to the harbour increased substantially. However, it would take new links with Scandinavia and the Baltic to bring major improvements to the port.

In 1780, engineer John Smeaton built the North Pier, increasing the water depth at the harbour entrance. Thomas Telford later extended the pier, adding the southern breakwater. Development continued during the 19th century with the addition of the Victoria Dock, Waterloo Quay, Matthews Quay and Blaikies Quay.

A wonderful example of the evolution of Aberdeen harbour can be seen on the North Pier, close to Pilot Square at Footdee. The Navigation Control Centre, an octagonal building, was built around 1798 as the Harbour Master's Station. Known as the Roundhouse, the distinctive building comprises a white-harled base with a steeply sloping slate roof that rises beyond an external balcony to a control tower. Harbour traffic was originally controlled by a signal involving three black balls mounted on a mast on the roof. In 1966 the signal was removed when the roof was raised to incorporate a new control tower.

Fun and food

For hundreds of years, Aberdeen and the fishing industry were inescapably linked as one. It is fitting therefore that one of the finest fish restaurants in the north-east of Scotland is right on the doorstep of the 'old fishing toon'. The Silver Darling Restaurant, located close to the Roundhouse, and named after the Scottish nickname for the herring, opened in 1986. The restaurant has been recommended in the Good Food Guide for more than 22 years and, in 2008, it was ranked by the Sunday Times as one of the top ten seafood restaurants in the UK. Owned by Frenchman Didier Dejean, the restaurant's menu consists largely of local fish, served with French and Mediterranean twists.

Leaving the seafood restaurant behind, and walking northwards from Footdee with the North Sea on the right, the view along the Esplanade is spectacular.

It is easy to understand why Aberdeen is affectionately known as the 'silver city

Amusement park

with the golden sands'. From this vantage point on the beachfront the golden sands seem to go on forever, with the bay curving around the local landscape.

After a short walk further along the Esplanade, a complete contrast to the old fishing village can be found, for at this point, the modern Esplanade comes into its own with its many new developments including a cinema, numerous restaurants, amusements, cafés and bars. This is the 21st-century side to Aberdeen beach.

Late into a summer's evening, whoops and screams can be heard from the thrills and spills of Sunset Boulevard. The pleasure park contains 26 ten-pin bowling lanes, dodgems, slot machines and numerous arcade-style adventures. Outside, there are several rollercoasters, including the Looping Star with its 360-degree loop. The Grampian Eye, a big wheel that stands 100 feet tall, offers excellent views over the harbour and across the sands.

After the hustle and bustle of the amusement park, attention might just turn to a nice cup of coffee. In this area of Aberdeen there is surely only one place to have such a treat, the Inversnecky Café.

Located on the beachfront, the Inversnecky opened for business in 1908 and still serves the best breakfast in town. First conceived by Lui Vicca, an Italian immigrant from Gaeta, close to Naples, the café has remained with the Vicca family ever since. The present-day owner, Martin Vicca, comments "Many people ask me about the name 'Inversnecky'. About 1926, when my grandfather took over the café from his father, there was a comedian called Harry Gordon who did summer shows at the local Gaiety Theatre, which was next door to the café. A lot of Harry's comedy characters were based on his fictitious Highland village of Inversnecky. My grandfather asked if Harry would object to him renaming the café the Inversnecky.

"Today the name Inversnecky is synony-mous with Aberdeen beach. I hear people say, 'let's go for an Inversnecky' when they really mean 'let's have a coffee'.

"Although we once catered for summer visitors, we now open all year. We specialise in breakfast and we have gained a great reputation for providing simple but good quality food. We use the best ingredients and we serve everything hot. Our coffee roast is a medium mocha, made from the finest Torelli beans.

"The quality of ingredients, together with an unquestionable desire to please our customers, is probably why we have become known for our food and coffee."

Of course, it is not just the Inversnecky that offers the thirsty explorer a place to stop for refreshment. There is a multitude of fast-food and chain restaurants within the arcade area, near to the cinema. Everything from traditional fish and chips to Chinese cuisine is available to replenish energy supplies, before continuing the journey along the city's beachfront.

Leisure and entertainment
Heading along the Esplanade from the amusement arcades and restaurants, the distinctive building you see beside the mini-roundabout at Links Road is the Aberdeen Beach Ballroom. An art deco building, which opened in 1929, it is home to one of Scotland's finest dance floors, which 'floats' on fixed steel springs.

Regularly hosting music, dance and sporting events, the Beach Ballroom has seen many prestigious visitors, including the Beatles, Pink Floyd, Cream and, more recently, The Ordinary Boys.

To the left of the Beach Ballroom, and dominating the landscape, is the Broad Hill, a favourite with those out for a Sunday stroll. The view from the top over the Esplanade is excellent. In 1832 the hill saw 40,000 people gathered on it to protest against Parliamentary and Burgh reforms. Another crowd gathered there in 1862, when some 30,000 people watched the very first Scottish Wapinschaw.

The Aberdeen Wapinschaw has a long history. The origins of this event lie in medieval times when every "man of any means" was expected to provide himself with arms and armour and to turn out when required to defend his country. A painting by Henry Pont, a local theatrical scene-painter, shows crowds surrounding the Broad Hill as some 2,500 regular soldiers and volunteers, wearing kilts and bearskins, marched with their guns and artillery, displaying their ability to take arms in readiness. Such was the popularity of the Aberdeen Wapinschaw that it became an annual event. Nowadays, it has evolved into a rifle-shooting contest and is held just outside Aberdeen at the Black Dog shooting range.

Just around the corner from the Broad Hill, on Constitution Street, is another example of exhibitionism. Satrosphere, billed as Scotland's first science and discovery centre, contains hands-on interactive exhibits and live shows that help to promote science in the community.

Satrosphere

enjoy a wonderful
cup of coffee on
the beachfront

savour local seafood
with a Mediterranean twist
at the Silver Darling
restaurant

stroll along
the golden sands
of Aberdeen Beach

meander around
the colour and
character of
Pilot Square,
'fittie'

Highlights

Opened in 1988, Satrosphere has gone from strength to strength. Lynsey Thompson, Development Manager at the centre, comments "Our popularity has grown because we really are a hands-on centre. We don't call ourselves a museum because that implies 'don't touch'. We are different, we want people to engage with science and for that to happen, people have to be able to get involved.

"We have lots of shows and workshops and we have daily demonstrations, which we call Science on the Spot. This involves one of our team going around the centre with a trolley, and engaging with people on the spot. It is great fun and a really good way to learn about science."

Satrosphere attracts over 50,000 visitors every year. With more than 50 interactive exhibits and special shows, there will almost certainly be something for everyone at the discovery centre. Lynsey adds "I have many favourite exhibits here but one of the most popular is called 'Slow Bubbles'. Basically, it's a cylindrical tube full of liquid silicone. There's a pump handle that allows you to pump air into the tube, creating bubbles. If you work quickly lots of small bubbles form, but these often merge into each other, creating interesting designs and structures.

"When I walk around the centre, I am always amazed, and excited, when I see crowds of children, and for that matter, adults, gathered around an exhibit. Although there is an element of entertainment in all our exhibits, having fun instils learning, and that is what we are all about. Our visitors can get involved, have fun and a laugh and at the same time learn something about the wonderful world of science."

Continuing along the Esplanade from the science discovery centre, the Beach Leisure Centre is worth a visit. The leisure pool is specially geared towards families, with its waves, a fountain and rapids. There are four exciting flumes to enjoy too.

Next door to the Beach Leisure Centre is one of Scotland's premier ice rinks. First opened in 1992, the Linx Ice Arena houses an ice pad and seating for over 1,000 spectators. The arena, which is open for public skating, hosts various ice-sport groups including the Aberdeen Ice Hockey Club and the Aberdeen Linx Figure Skating Club.

From the buildings of the Beach Ballroom, Aberdeen Leisure Centre and the ice arena, the area running parallel with the beachfront continues with the sporting theme, but it is golf that now dominates. The King's Links, a municipal golf course, has a wide range of holes to test the

Breakers on the beach

most experienced golfer. The changeable weather conditions, together with the strong winds that often whip off the sea, make this course an exciting challenge.

On the opposite side of the road that divides the Esplanade, the golden sands are ever present. Regardless of weather, there will always be people enjoying a walk along the wide pavements that sweep around the distinctive bay. Perhaps it is the melodic sound from the constant crashing of the energetic waves that makes this an appealing place to walk.

The beach suffers from sand erosion, so a feature that makes the beach stand out from other local beaches are the groynes, installed in the early 20th century to absorb some of the energy from the waves and to slow down sand movement. In a more recent attempt to reduce erosion, 100,000 tonnes of sand were shipped from further down the coast and sprayed onto the beach. In addition, tonnes of rocks were laid in a v-shape to help absorb some of the energy from the sea, thus reducing further sand movement.

For many people a gentle stroll in the peace and tranquillity at the edge of the sea is all that is needed. But for those who like to enjoy a little more energetic pastime there are ample opportunities here. On most days of the year wind-surfers can be seen launching themselves from the shore to catch a breaking wave, while fishing enthusiasts cast their lines in the hope of cod, pollack or coalfish.

Nature reserve

At the far end of the Esplanade, near to the mouth of the River Don, an abundance of wildlife awaits the intrepid explorer. Ian Talboys, an officer from the Countryside Ranger Service, comments "Donmouth, which is at the northern end of Aberdeen beach, is a great place to witness nature in action. This area of the Esplanade is dynamic. The continual inter-action between the waters coming down the river and those of the North Sea make the Donmouth such a fascinating place to visit. The erosion and deposition of sand and silt by the river and sea have created and moulded an estuary that is home to an abundance of plants and animals.

"At low tide the mudflats are home to red-shanks, black and white oystercatchers, common and sandwich terns and gannets. Many birds migrate to this area during the winter months, particularly from Northern Europe and Scandinavia, while others come to us for the summer months. Common terns will often be seen flying acrobatically along the river, diving from 20 feet into the water to catch a fish. Sometimes we get visits from warblers that have been blown off-track from their migratory routes through Eastern Europe. It is a very interesting place."

Designated a Local Nature Reserve in 1992, this end of the Esplanade is in complete contrast to the opposite end at Footdee. Within a two-and-a-half-mile stretch of city beach, the landscape changes from historic fishing village, with its own unique micro-culture, to a nature reserve that is rich in beauty and wildlife. In between there is everything from thrills and spills of fast-moving rollercoasters to the freshness of the gentle spray from the sea.

Regardless of time of year, this part of the city is always busy and is well worth a visit. Whether it be to enjoy a stroll during the long summer evenings or to plunge into the chilly North Sea, a visit to Aberdeen is not complete until the Esplanade has been explored. And above all, a nice cup of coffee awaits those willing to make the journey.

Exploring

The Silver Darling Restaurant

The Silver Darling, called after the Scottish nickname for the herring, is owned and run by Frenchman Didier Dejean. His menus consist largely of local fish served with a French twist, and a Mediterranean and occasional Far Eastern flourish.

On a fine summer's evening, sit back and watch the sunset over Aberdeen harbour while enjoying the finest seafood in the north-east of Scotland.

The restaurant is located on the North Pier at Footdee.
www.thesilverdarling.co.uk

Codona's

Codona's Sunset Boulevard, which is open 364 days a year, offers fun and entertainment for the whole family. The team at Codona's has taken the art of 'eat, drink and play' to a whole new level. There are 26 ten-pin bowling lanes, pool tables and bar areas, all with giant projection screens where music and sports videos are played.

Codona's Amusement Park has a range of thrills and spills to be enjoyed, from the Looping Star rollercoaster with its 360-degree loop, to the new Vertigo Aerial Assault Course.
www.codonas.com

Inversnecky

Founded in 1908 by Italian Lui Vicca, who left his home in Gaeta near Naples to seek his fortune, the Inversnecky Café has become a local legend. The family has built a reputation on serving quality food and coffee at a reasonable price.

Current owner, Martin Vicca, says "Perhaps the best testimonial to the quality of food that we offer is that people are willing to wait during busy times for a table. Whether you are looking for a full breakfast, a slice of homemade cake or a great cup of coffee, you can be sure of a friendly and welcoming experience."
www.inversnecky.co.uk

Satrosphere

Satrosphere is Scotland's first science and discovery centre. With hands-on interactive exhibits and live science shows, a visit to Satrosphere will not only inspire the scientist within but will also entertain the whole family.

After engaging with the numerous exhibits, relax and unwind in the Tramshed Coffee House, which is situated next to the science centre. It is a warm and welcoming venue, serving modern coffee.

Satrosphere is about a ten-minute walk from the city centre. From Castlegate, head along Justice Street and then onto Park Street. Continue along Park Street to Constitution Street.

For opening times and other information, visit the Satrosphere website.
www.satrosphere.net

Aberdeen Beach Leisure Centre

There is something for everyone at Aberdeen's beachfront leisure complex. The pool has many water features, including four flumes. The centre boasts a double-sized sports hall equipped for virtually every indoor game, and there is even a challenging indoor climbing wall.

Crèche facilities are available within the centre and there is a café for refreshments and light meals.
www.aberdeencity.gov.uk/sportaberdeen

Linx Ice Arena

The Linx Ice Arena is one of Scotland's premier ice rinks. It was first opened for public use in February 1992 and operates every day of the year except Christmas and New Year's Day.

The ice arena facility consists of an ice pad with spectator seating for over 1,000 people.

There is a cafeteria within the facility, which is open at weekends.
www.aberdeencity.gov.uk/sportaberdeen

King's Links Golf Club

The King's Links 18-hole golf course is a traditional, well-established links course, running parallel to the Aberdeen beachfront and close to other leisure facilities, and to Pittodrie Stadium, home of Aberdeen Football Club. The course has a wide range of holes, the longest being 502 yards, with the shortest a 171-yard par 3.

The King's Links Golf Club is located off Golf Road, opposite Pittodrie Stadium.
www.aberdeencity.gov.uk/sportaberdeen

Donmouth Local Nature Reserve

The Donmouth Local Nature Reserve is two miles north of the centre of Aberdeen, on King Street. There is plenty of roadside parking on the north end of the Esplanade, which is off King Street on the right at the Bridge of Don.

The best way to explore the Donmouth is to walk a circuit from the Esplanade up to the Brig o' Balgownie, cross the brig and return on the other side of the river. If visiting by car, park on the Esplanade, about 100 feet from the Bridge of Don. After enjoying the estuary, the beach and mudflats, walk towards the bridge. Cross King Street at the lights and take the footpath on the left bank of the river. Watch out for seals that may be visiting the little island just past the Bridge of Don.
www.aberdeencity.gov.uk

Other venues

In addition to the venues mentioned above, there are numerous other entertainment and eating venues along the Esplanade. From fast-food outlets, restaurants, a cinema and other coffee shops, the choice along the beachfront is varied.

ART, ARTISTS AND GALLERIES

Aberdeen has a long association with art. The city is much richer for its strong and vibrant connections with creativity, from the 16th-century portrait artist George Jameson to contemporary painters and print-makers. Art and artists play an important role in the life and heart of the city, providing an abundance of opportunities for the cultural explorer.

Aberdeen Art Gallery is the largest public gallery in the north of Scotland. Attracting more than 200,000 visitors each year, the gallery houses one of the most important collections in the country, from 18th-century portraits by Raeburn to powerful 20th-century works by Paul Nash and Francis Bacon. Paintings include excellent examples of French Impressionists Monet, Renoir, Sisley and Degas, and of Post-Impressionist Toulouse-Lautrec.

Opened in 1885, the origins of the gallery can be traced to 1873, when three public-spirited local men put money, energy and influence into opening an art gallery for the public. These were granite merchant Alexander MacDonald, flour merchant John Forbes White, and Sir George Reid.

George Reid, born in Aberdeen in 1841, was himself an artist. When he was 13, he was appointed to Messrs Keith & Gibb, lithographers, of Aberdeen. His apprenticeship lasted for seven years, after which time he took art lessons from an itinerant portrait painter, William Niddrie.

Reid moved to Edinburgh where he studied at the school of the Board of Trustees, known as the Trustees' Academy, now Edinburgh College of Art. He returned to Aberdeen some time afterwards, to paint landscapes and portraits for, as the *Encyclopaedia Britannica* records, "any trifling sum which his work could command".

One of George Reid's first portraits to attract attention was that of George MacDonald, the poet and novelist. The painting is now the property of the University of Aberdeen.

During his early years, Reid was supported by local businessman and art collector John Forbes White. Together with another businessman, Alexander MacDonald, the three formed a committee with other city fathers, and, in 1885, Aberdeen Art Gallery was opened.

Designed by architect Alexander Marshall Mackenzie, who also designed Marischal

College in Aberdeen and the Waldorf Hotel in London, the gallery is built around a magnificent centre court with grey and rose granite columns. Together with its bright and contemporary café and gallery shop, the venue is an important part of the city's culture.

Jennifer Melville, Curator at Aberdeen Art Gallery, comments "The gallery began originally as a fine art and industrial museum and the emphasis has always been on collecting contemporary and modern art. That's because our first benefactors bought contemporary art directly from the artist rather than through an agent or intermediary: they liked to know the artist. That traditionally is really what distinguishes this gallery from lots of others.

"We have a significant collection of applied art as well, including ceramics, costume, furniture, glass, jewellery, metalwork and textiles. The impressive James McBey Print Room, built in memory of the celebrated local artist, houses a large collection of prints, drawings and photographs.

"One of the most popular aspects of the gallery is its exciting programme of special exhibitions and events, created from the city's permanent collections. We also have a good selection of touring exhibitions from home and abroad.

These all help to engage our visitors with contemporary art."

Contemporary art in Aberdeen

The contemporary art scene in Aberdeen was given another boost around the same time that the art gallery was established. Local businessman and philanthropist, John Gray, offered to finance and build a new school of science and art in the city. Rising from humble beginnings as a carpenter, Gray became a partner in a local firm of engineers and iron founders. In 1859 he was appointed director of the Aberdeen Mechanics Institution, a forerunner of what is now Robert Gordon University.

Gray wanted his new school to be sited next to Aberdeen Art Gallery, to give architectural coherence to the area. In 1885, the same year as the gallery opened, Gray's School of Science and Art was founded.

Now one of Scotland's major art schools, Gray's is home to 200 undergraduate fine art students and 500 students studying design.

Allan Watson, Head of Fine Art, says "Contemporary art is an important part of Aberdeen's culture. Since the formation of Aberdeen Art Gallery and Gray's School of Art, Aberdeen has become, not only an important centre for modern art, but also

Returning to the harbour, by Ricky Robb

check out
North East Open Studios
and explore the work
of local artists,
photographers and
sculptors

browse the Captains
Paintings and enjoy
the story of
maritime evolution
in Aberdeen

visit Aberdeen Art Gallery, see the permanent collections and browse the latest exhibitions

follow the Sculpture Trail to see traditional and modern commemorative pieces

Highlights

a place where local artists are not afraid to push the boundaries of conventional thinking.

"Our students are hugely serious, committed and passionate about their work. Many of them will go on to form excellent exhibitions that can be enjoyed by local people and people who are visiting the city. You just have to look around the town and you will see lots of great galleries, from the public art gallery to numerous private galleries, each promoting their form of contemporary art."

Emerging artists

Limousine Bull is a great example of an artists' collective that operates success-fully within the city. Formed in 1998, the collective is run by a committee and funded by grants and private donations. Their 'mobile' exhibitions attract locals and visitors who are interested in exploring cutting-edge creativity.

Manager of Limousine Bull, and herself a graduate from Gray's School of Art, Carrie Ginniver comments "Our objective is to bring contemporary art to an audience within Aberdeen. Although there are several private art galleries within the city, we are one of a small number that are publically funded. That gives us the opportunity to be at the forefront of presenting modern art to the public.

"We provide artists with a platform to showcase their work, creating in turn a unique art scene within the city. There are many traditional artists operating in and around Aberdeen, who do very well with their work. However, through the work of Limousine Bull, we are able to provide artists with an opportunity to explore social, political and environmental issues surrounding the north-east of Scotland.

"I think we are starting to cross a bridge that we've never crossed before. There are a lot of really exciting artists emerging through the local school, and through our gallery, who will be able to break into the national and international art scene. Not only does that provide opportunities for individual artists, but it provides a great and vibrant art culture within the city, for local people and for visitors to explore and enjoy."

Galleries

Established in 1974, Peacock Visual Arts is another important organisation in Aberdeen. Located just off the Castlegate, Peacock's main aim is to nurture a culture of creativity in the city.

Peacock is located in two buildings on Castle Street, part of a city conservation area. The gallery, where national and international print-makers exhibit their work, was originally built in 1710. Across the narrow street the workshops, built

Street by Stuart Edwards, Limousine Bull

as a school in 1860, house a wide range of print-making equipment for screen-printing, mono-printing, etching, lithography and relief-printing.

Peacock Visual Arts is not just about providing workshops for artists to use. It is also about bringing artists and the public together, so that both can engage, explore and share ideas that provide stimulation and challenge for artists and the public.

Presenting contemporary art to stimulate and excite the local population and the visitor has its challenges. "There is a strong tradition of art in the north-east of Scotland," says Maura Tighe, owner of Gallery Heinzel in Aberdeen's west end. "I think it is probably because of the excellent art school in the city, and probably because the local population know what they like.

"At Heinzel, we represent about 80 artists from around Scotland, so our gallery produces a good cross-section of work. There is definitely a north-east bias but it is not exclusive.

"Aberdeen has a great selection of galleries to visit, from the excellent public gallery to several privately owned art spaces. I think the number of galleries reflects the importance that art plays in terms of public interest and in terms of the culture of the city.

"In fact, this area has one of Scotland's largest open studios event. Every year, artists, photographers, print-makers and galleries in the north-east open their doors to the public. I am not sure how many artists participate in this event but I do know that it probably runs to over 200 people. These include artists who paint very traditional landscapes, to people who specialise in multi-media to jewellery makers, ceramic workers and pinhole photographers. I think the sheer number of artists who participate in this scheme is testament to the fact that the north-east and Aberdeen offer so many opportunities for creative people.

"There is something really exciting about the local landscape, which presents a great challenge for the artist. I think it is the light around this area. Often the light is much flatter than, say, the west coast of Scotland. Our artists here at Heinzel capture the mood and essence of the local environment, usually in the abstract form. We find that people who come into our gallery are immediately able to associate with the colours, mood and atmosphere that our artists have created."

Atmosphere and mood, in particular the wild and angry sea, are exactly the things that inspire the vibrant work of one local artist, Helen Bruce. The changing characteristics that the sea and the local landscape offer have become a passion

Sketch of the Town House, by Martin Ferguson

for Helen. She says "The sea is at its most vibrant when it is wild and angry – it throws up such unique colours and it changes so quickly from one mood to another.

"Capturing mood isn't easy, it is challenging. Painting in the abstract form helps me to communicate much more about the changing environment than simply painting a representation of it."

Helen's use of colour helps her express the dynamic nature of the landscapes around the north-east of Scotland. "Many people say to me that I shouldn't use such a wide range of colour in my work. But if you look carefully at the sky in this area of Scotland, you will see that it contains all the colours of the rainbow."

Although Helen paints in the abstract form, she likes to include a familiar element in each image. This might be a recognisable horizon, a striking sky, or a path leading into the distance. Often she will use a strong diagonal through her paintings, such as a fence or wall. It is these reference points that create stability, almost taking the image from a true abstraction to a more 'user-friendly' style.

Helen especially likes the juxtaposition that the coastline offers the artist in this area of Scotland. She says "There is a feeling of safeness when standing on top of the cliffs around here, yet when you start to walk down a path towards the sea, you leave behind the safe area, venturing into danger.

"This area is full of drama. You only have to look at how fields are separated by fences, old and new, or look at ploughed fields, or tiny villages nestling in hollows, and you will see drama.

"Nature reminds me to be respectful of the junction where land meets sea. Powerful energy, serene and moody shapes, colours in abundance and texture picked out by the ever-changing light – what more is there to fuel the emotions of both painter and art enthusiast alike?"

The city and the sea

Of course, it is not only present-day artists who capture the drama of the seas around Aberdeen. In 1888 David Farquharson, originally from Blairgowrie, painted *The Herring Fleet Leaving the Dee*. This painting highlighted the important role the harbour played in the development of the city. The image, which is on display at the Aberdeen Maritime Museum, encapsulates a vital era in Aberdeen's maritime history.

Another fine example of early maritime art is the painting of the schooner *Smithfield*, by Arthur Smith (1814–82), which is

Sand dunes at the beach

on display at Aberdeen Maritime Museum. The vessel, built around 1842 at the Duthie Shipyard, was owned by the Aberdeen Lime Company and was used to carry coal, lime and manure along the east coast, often from Aberdeen to London. Cattle were also carried on these ships, to the London meat markets. *Smithfield* caught fire at sea in 1875, while bringing lime to Aberdeen. The crew managed to coax the badly damaged ship into port.

Both these paintings, together with many other excellent examples of 'Captains' paintings' can be viewed at the Aberdeen Maritime Museum. Telling the story of the city's long relationship with the sea, this award-winning museum houses a unique collection of art and other items covering shipbuilding, fishing and port history.

Provost Ross' House, which is now part of the Maritime Museum, was built in 1593 by master-mason Andrew Jamieson. The house became the residence of Provost John Ross who was himself a ship-owner.

During the 19th century, the building was divided into domestic housing units but was reduced to a derelict condition by the 1950s. The house was acquired by the National Trust for Scotland and then leased to Aberdeen City Council in 1984, when it became the Aberdeen Maritime Museum.

A few years after the opening, a neighbouring church was purchased with a view to extending the museum. After a five-year period, which involved architects, museum designers and curators, the present-day museum opened in May 1997.

Now housing a unique collection of past and present sea-going memorabilia, including a 27-foot-high model of the Murchison oil platform, the museum, one of the city's main tourist attractions, has won a host of awards. These include Scottish Museum of the Year, the Supreme Award in Regeneration, the Aberdeen Civic Award, and the Best Building category at the Scottish Architectural Awards.

Together with the unique collections of art in the Aberdeen Maritime Museum, public art collections in Aberdeen include more than 15,000 items. From exciting fine art collections that are of local, national and international significance, to collections of applied art, design, craft, costumes and textiles, the city is truly an art-lovers paradise. Not only are the public galleries filled with exciting collections of past and present contemporary paintings, the numerous high-quality private galleries display work that captures the essence of the city, its vibrancy, drama and ever-changing climatic conditions that make this part of the north-east of Scotland a visual heaven.

Impressions of the Don, by Donna Morrison

Exploring

Aberdeen Art Gallery

Aberdeen Art Gallery is located on Schoolhill, just off Union Street. The gallery, open each day except Mondays, has a shop where a unique range of jewellery, stationery, cards, books and crafts can be purchased. There is a bright and contemporary child-friendly coffee shop that features Fair Trade produce.
www.aagm.co.uk

The Rendezvous Gallery

The Rendezvous Gallery has become a familiar landmark in the west end of Aberdeen. Originally opened in 1975, the owners have become highly experienced and knowledgeable in Scottish art. The Rendezvous Gallery presents around 10 exhibitions every year, usually solo shows by Scottish contemporary artists.
www.rendezvous-gallery.co.uk

Gallery Heinzel

Gallery Heinzel specialises in contemporary Scottish art from its base in Thistle Street, at the Holburn end of Union Street. Its bright and modern premises are filled with continually changing exhibitions of work by some of the 80 artists whom the gallery represents.
www.galleryheinzel.com

North East Open Studios

Formed in 2003, the North East Open Studios (NEOS) event was primarily set up to provide an opportunity for artists to reach out to the public around the north-east and to provide the public with access to the hundreds of artists who operate around the area.

NEOS has gone from strength to strength, winning the Northern Lights Tourism Award in 2007 for Best Aberdeenshire Tourism Initiative. Every September, over 250 artists and gallery owners open their studios to the public.
www.northeastopenstudios.co.uk

Peacock Visual Arts

Peacock is the leading contemporary visual arts organisation in Aberdeen. The centre aims to bring artists and the public together through exhibitions, events, talks, residences, film screenings, gigs and workshops, to make and present art in exciting and innovative ways. With a fantastic range of courses on offer, all led by experienced tutors at the well-equipped workshop, the facility is open to beginners and advanced artists alike. Bookbinding, screen-printing, relief-printing and etching are some of the many courses on offer.
www.peacockvisualarts.com

Gray's Degree Show

Every year, usually in June, Robert Gordon University holds a student degree show. This annual event, a highlight in the city's art calendar, showcases the work of graduating students. Many students who become leading names in the national and international art scene had their first opportunity to exhibit their work at the Gray's Degree Show.
www.rgu.ac.uk

Aberdeen Maritime Museum

The Aberdeen Maritime Museum tells the story of the city's long relationship with the sea. This award-winning museum is located on the historic Shiprow, and incorporates Provost Ross' House, built in 1593.

The Maritime Museum houses a unique collection of art and other memorabilia covering shipbuilding, fast sailing ships, fishing and port history. It is the only place in the UK where the story of North Sea oil is told.

The museum, open every day except Mondays, offers the visitor a spectacular viewpoint over the busy harbour.
www.aagm.co.uk

The Hamnavoe Gallery

The Hamnavoe Gallery is located in the city's west end, on Fonthill Road. The name Hamnavoe comes from the old Norse word for Stromness in Orkney, meaning 'heaven in the bay'. The gallery, opened in 2005, exhibits some of the best in Scottish art.

Sculpture Trail

Aberdeen's city centre has a diverse range of sculptures. These range from traditional to contemporary, and perform many functions, such as commemoration, memorial and remembrance, and the expression of ideas. An excellent guide to city-centre sculptures is available from the Aberdeen City Council website.
www.aberdeencity.gov.uk

The Milton Gallery

About 15 miles west of Aberdeen, on the A93, near Milton of Crathes, is the Milton Gallery. Located in a renovated steading, the gallery is home to a number of local and national artists. With constantly changing exhibitions, the gallery has gained a formidable reputation as a place for the serious art enthusiast to visit.
www.miltonart.com

Limousine Bull

The artists' collective, Limousine Bull, is located at various venues throughout the city. For information about the latest exhibitions, visit their website.
www.limousinebull.org.uk

A BIKE RIDE AROUND THE CITY

Aberdeen city centre is quite compact, allowing easy access on foot to many of the historical and entertainment attractions. However, there is much more to the city than the inner urban area. For example, the Kincorth Nature Reserve, just four miles from Union Street, is picturesque and has lots of wildlife, and the scenery of the coastal trail, famous for its links with Aberdeen's maritime heritage, is dramatic, beautiful and romantic. One of the best ways of exploring these outlying areas is to hire a bike and cycle the Aberdeen cycle trail.

The Esplanade at Aberdeen's beachfront is a great place to start the cycle trail, if for no other reason than it is an ideal place to arrange collection of a hire bike. There is plenty of car-parking, which is free.

Running for over two and a half miles, and starting from the Donmouth Local Nature Reserve at the north end, the Esplanade has a wide carriageway and a speed limit, in some parts, of 15 mph, making it ideal for trying out a hire bike and for getting to grips with its handling.

With the golden sands of the beach on the left and the King's Links Golf Course on the right, and with the usual gentle breeze coming off the sea, cycling along

the Esplanade is a pleasant experience. Cycle for a few minutes, enjoying the scenery, before passing the amusement and arcade centre. Whoops and screams will often be heard from Codona's Amusement Park, where the Looping Star rollercoaster propels passengers through a 360-degree loop.

The trail continues towards the southern end of the Esplanade to Footdee – locally known as Fittie. Although this area of the city has been inhabited since medieval times, the present-day layout was first constructed during the 19th century, to house the influx of fishing families from around the north-east to the flourishing harbour area of Aberdeen.

In terms of traffic, the busiest part of the Aberdeen cycle trail runs from the end of the Esplanade until it reaches the other side of Victoria Bridge. Good road sense and a keen lookout for other road-users are essential during the whole trail, but nowhere more so than during this section. However, this busy part only runs for two miles so it is worth coping with the heavy traffic because after this section the trail gets much quieter.

Once a burgh in its own right, Torry, lying on the south bank of the River Dee, was

Breakwater at Aberdeen Harbour

incorporated into the City of Aberdeen in 1891 after the construction of the Victoria Bridge. The bridge, built after a ferry disaster that claimed the lives of 32 people, became an important link between Torry and the more populous centre of Aberdeen.

Maritime heritage

After crossing Victoria Bridge, the trail turns first left onto South Esplanade East and then left again onto Sinclair Road. During the early 1960s, significant oil and gas reserves were discovered in the North Sea. Oil companies started to explore those reserves and Aberdeen found itself in the early stages of what would become a world centre of excellence for oil and gas production. Most of this area of Torry was transformed during the 1970s. Supply vessels, used to transport supplies and equipment to the oil production platforms, replaced the fishing boats that once lined the harbour around Torry. The oil industry had arrived in Aberdeen.

Moving away from the hustle and bustle of the busy oil capital of Europe, the cycle trail leads onto the quieter Greyhope Road. Stop the bike here and take a few moments to enjoy the spectacular view over the city of Aberdeen. The entire harbour, Victoria Bridge and the lower reaches of the River Dee can all be seen. On a clear day it is even possible to see the whole of the Esplanade and the golden sands of Aberdeen beach as the bay curves into the horizon.

Cycling further along Greyhope Road, with the Balnagask Golf Course on the right, the most noticeable sight on the left side are the two breakwaters. Engineer Thomas Telford proposed building the breakwaters in the early 19th century, to combat the effects of siltation at the harbour entrance. The main breakwater, the larger of the two south breakwaters and made from concrete, was constructed between 1869 and 1874.

Before leaving the harbour it is perhaps poignant to reflect on its murkier past. As in many coastal cities around Scotland, the child slave trade was both rife and, for many business people, very lucrative here. Peter Williamson, a local lad from Aboyne, a small village to the west of Aberdeen, has a tale that is a familiar one. When he was 13 he went to live with his aunt in Aberdeen. However, employees of unscrupulous businessmen including James Elphinstone, John Burnett and Walter Cochrane snatched him at the harbour. These were men of high standing in the city; some of them were also local magistrates.

Children were kidnapped and held in various buildings around the city centre, until a ship was ready to take them to America. Local legend has it that the

'barn', a 16th-century house in the Green, held up to 50 boys while they awaited transportation. Fiddlers and other musicians would be hired to play and drown out the cries from the boys.

Peter Williamson was taken across the Atlantic on the ship *The Planter*, which was wrecked off the coast of America. He was sold to a fellow Scot, Hugh Wilson, who himself had been kidnapped as a boy. When Hugh died, Peter was free from his indenture. He went on to lead an exciting life in America, being captured by Indians and later fighting in the Indian and French wars. He was captured and returned to Britain in the 1750s as a prisoner-of-war.

After writing a book about his experiences, Peter Williamson was arrested when he returned to Aberdeen to sell his work. The magistrates in Aberdeen claimed that he was guilty of libel and, following a quick trial, certain pages of his book were ordered to be torn out and burned by the local hangman at the mercat cross.

Peter was banished from Aberdeen, so he went to live in Edinburgh. He continued to fight against the magistrates in Aberdeen and it was during his struggle to bring justice that witnesses began to come forward. Margaret Ross, mother of James, told of her son being taken by people who worked for local merchant

Alexander Gray. After many years struggling with the justice system Peter finally managed to bring a halt to the slave-trading of young boys. Peter died in Edinburgh in 1799. It is not known when the practice of kidnapping stopped in Aberdeen, but it probably did not survive much beyond the late 1750s.

On the right-hand side, as the Greyhope Road leaves the harbour behind, is the old defensive post, the Torry Battery. Construction of the battery began in 1859 and was completed in March 1861. First manned by volunteers, the forerunners of the Territorial Army, the defensive post was armed with nine heavy Armstrong 200-pound guns. These have been described as being capable of "dropping a ball from Torry as far as Newburgh" (a small village about ten miles north of the city). In 1904, the gunners of Torry Battery won the King's Cup at the Scottish National Artillery Association Competition for their ability to shoot with accuracy.

During the First World War, Torry Battery was manned on a permanent basis and used as a training ground. Although not manned after the war, the guns remained.

Additional artillery was added to the battery during the Second World War, mainly because of the threat from German dive-bombers and to protect the city from attacks by sea. On the night of 3 June

1941 the guns of Torry Battery opened fire when two unidentified vessels were seen approaching the harbour.

After the war, there was little need for a harbour defence system so partial demolition of Torry Battery took place during the 1950s, but was never completed. Today, the remains can be seen high on the Greyhope peninsula.

A few hundred feet further on from the Torry Battery, is the Girdleness Lighthouse. Designed by Robert Stevenson, grandfather of the writer Robert Louis Stevenson, the lighthouse was first lit in 1833. It was an important navigation mark to alert ships to the danger of the wave-cut platform that extends right across the Girdleness peninsula. In 1813 a whaling ship called *Oscar* foundered on the rocks. From a crew of 43, sadly, only three people survived the tragedy. This prompted the building of the lighthouse.

The cycle route now leads along the picturesque old coast road, past Doonies Farm on the right. Covering more than 130 acres, the farm is a member of the Rare Breeds Survival Trust and is one of only two farms in Scotland to be awarded Approved Conservation Farm Park status. Amongst the animals at the farm are examples of Norfolk Horn sheep, Golden Guernsey goats, Whiteface Woodland rams and Eriskay ponies. Other animals include

poultry – hens, cockerels and ducks.

A city nature reserve

Turning right onto Hareness Road, near to the old bridge under the railway line on the left, the cycle trail runs through Altens Industrial Estate. After crossing the roundabout at Wellington Road, a left turn takes the trail onto Tollohill Drive, with the Kincorth Hill Local Nature Reserve on the left.

Kincorth Hill, known locally as Kinkers, has been managed as a Local Nature Reserve since 1997. It is a haven for wildlife and provides excellent views over the city and surrounding countryside. The name Kincorth comes from Celtic, meaning 'head of the moor'. In 1178, King William the Lion gifted the lands of Kincorth to Arbroath Abbey and the monks rented out the land for sheep grazing. However, during the Reformation of the Church in 1587, the Crown took back ownership of the land.

In the 17th century, King Charles I wanted to take control of the Scottish Church. However, the League of Covenanters opposed the king and, in 1639, a famous victory by the Covenanters was won when an army, camped at Kincorth Hill, fought and defeated the king's men at the Battle of the Dee.

Many years later, Kincorth Hill was to provide a rich source of building material to send to England. In 1766 quarrying at the hill was started, with stone being transported by cart to Torry Pier where ships would take it to London to be used for paving and building. The last quarry closed after the Second World War and the deep excavations were filled in with domestic waste and covered with soil.

Large areas of Kincorth Hill were planted with pine, spruce and larch in the 1980s. Gorse scrub covers a large part of the hill and provides an abundance of colour during the summertime. In fact, it is often the bright yellow of Kincorth Hill that catches the eye of motorists as they enter the city from the south.

Wildflowers such as yellow rattle, knapweed and cow parsley flourish at the nature reserve in summer. It is home to a diverse range of insects and birds, such as the small copper butterfly and the meadow pipit bird.

Suburbs

From the tranquillity and beauty of the nature reserve, the Aberdeen cycle trail leads down from the hill to the River Dee, crossing the King George VI Bridge. The foundation stone of the bridge was laid in September 1938 by the then Lord Provost of Aberdeen, Provost Edward W Watt, and the bridge was opened in 1941 by the queen, in the presence of King George VI. The provost is a figurative and ceremonial head of a principal city in Scotland. Each of the four main cities, Aberdeen, Edinburgh, Glasgow and Dundee, has a right to appoint a Lord Provost instead of a provost (a mayor).

After crossing the bridge, the trail heads west along Riverside Drive until it reaches the Bridge of Dee, where it continues onto Garthdee Road, Inchgarth Road and then into the suburb of Cults. The Bridge of Dee is one of Aberdeen's finest landmarks. The 'brig o' Dee', which dates from 1527, was the site of the battle between the Royalists and the Covenanters. At a height of 30 feet above the waterline, the bridge, which is now a nationally important Scheduled Monument, consists of seven nearly semi-circular ribbed arches built from granite.

The cycle trail skirts around the western periphery of Aberdeen. Travelling along Kirk Brae past Hazlehead Golf Course, the quiet road cuts through forests and farmland and leads past Kingswells, then over to Newhills before a steep descent takes the trail back into the city at Bucksburn.

The River Don estuary

start the journey
and admire the view
on the beachfront

cycle some of the
wonderful paths around
Kincorth Hill and enjoy
the view of the city

take a break at Doonies
Farm to watch the rare
breeds

stop for lunch or
a snack at one of
the many fine eating
places in Cults

Highlights

Formerly a market village, Bucksburn, named after a stream that flows through it, has been swallowed up by the spread of the city and is now unrecognisable as a separate suburb.

Bucksburn adjoins another area, Bridge of Don, by Mugiemoss Road. Synonymous with paper-making, the area of Mugiemoss has a vibrant history. Charles Davidson, son of a farmer from Tarland, Aberdeen-shire, set up the mill at Mugiemoss in 1811, leasing land for £18 per annum. The mill initially produced snuff. Paper-making came later, probably around 1820, with the business passing from father to sons in 1843 after Charles died. The company thrived, becoming a major employer of local people. However in 2005 the mill, after almost 200 years of production, closed.

From Mugiemoss Road, the trail crosses the River Don, over the Persely Bridge, and leads through one of the largest city suburbs in Europe. Known simply as the 'brig o' Don', with a population of over 20,000 people, the area grew rapidly to accommodate the expansion in population as a result of the oil industry boom.

Before returning to the Esplanade, the Aberdeen cycle trail passes one more important landmark in the city, Glover House. Thomas Blake Glover, who was born in Aberdeenshire but later moved with his family to Aberdeen, is today revered in Japan as one of the founders of modern Japan. He had a crucial role in the industrialisation of the country and in the introduction of western developments into manufacturing.

Glover formed his own company in Japan in the early 1860s, becoming a merchant for ships, guns and gunpowder. His business was based in Nagasaki and it was here that he built his home, the first western-style building in Japan. His association with the samurai clans gained him the nickname, the Scottish Samurai. He was also credited with bringing the first steam railway locomotive, called the Iron Duke, to the country.

And so the Aberdeen cycle trail returns to its starting point on the Esplanade – a route that provides diversity in both cycling and in history, from beginning to end. It is fitting that the journey starts and ends near the sea, for it is water that has dominated the evolution of Aberdeen, whether it be the harbour or the two rivers that cut through city life. The cycle trail runs through areas that are steeped in maritime history and legend, through picturesque settings such as Kincorth Hill and back amidst the industrial revolution of paper-making, through to oil and gas production. Cycling around Aberdeen is a great way to truly witness the diversity that exists in this exquisite Scottish city.

Exploring

The Aberdeen cycle trail

The Aberdeen cycle trail is 28 miles long, starting and finishing on the Esplanade at Aberdeen beach. Although the route has been given a designated starting point it is possible to start anywhere along the trail. However, the Esplanade is an ideal place to start and finish because there is ample car-parking in the area and it is a convenient place for bike hire companies to drop off and pick up cycles.

The cycle trail is fairly easy riding, with few steep sections. At an average speed of around ten miles per hour, and allowing time for stops, it is possible to complete the route in about five hours. However, the trail has been divided into six shorter routes.

These shorter sections, all of which return to the Esplanade, range from a six-mile route along the coastal road, to a 14-mile section that takes in Kincorth Hill and the Bridge of Dee before returning to the city.

There are many places on the trail to stop for food and refreshments. There are several cafés on the Esplanade and in the harbour area. However, the section along the coast, from Greyhope Road to Kincorth Hill, has limited places to stop for food. This is a long section, and food and drink should be taken for this part of the journey.

After descending from Kincorth Hill onto Riverside Drive, there are several places to buy food near to the Bridge of Dee, including supermarkets and petrol stations. Further along the route, in Cults, there are several cafés and bakeries. However, there is another long section after Cults with few places to eat, so again food and drink should be taken.

With all cycling on public roads, care must be taken. The route starts on the relatively quiet streets of the Esplanade, but soon moves to busier roads, particularly around Market Street. Great care is needed during this section as heavy traffic can build up, including lorries and other commercial vehicles.

Once over the Torry Bridge, the trail does get much quieter.

It is recommended that bicycles used for this route, or for any other cycling in Aberdeen, are in good condition. There are several bike hire companies that provide excellent mountain and road bikes. In addition to the bike, other equipment should be carried including tyre repair kits, spare inner tubes, food and drink, money and, if possible, a mobile telephone in case of emergency. Adequate clothing, suitable for the weather conditions, should be taken as well as a cycle helmet.

Although it is possible to complete the entire trail in one journey, many people prefer to tackle only one or two sections at a time. A map showing the entire trail and all the shorter loops can be downloaded from the *15 things to do* website.
www.15thingstodo.com/cycleaberdeen

It should be noted that the Aberdeen cycle trail is not marked on the roadway, nor are there signposts along the way. The route has been carefully selected for the purposes of this publication and is not part of a recognised national or local cycling route, nor has the route been endorsed by the local council nor by any cycling association.

Cycling advice
Excellent advice about cycling in Aberdeen can be obtained from the Aberdeen City Council website.
www.aberdeencity.gov.uk

The UK's National Cyclists' Organisation (CTC), the UK's largest cycling charity, promotes safe cycling around the country. The Aberdeen branch of the CTC has an active membership and welcomes newcomers.
www.ctc.org.uk
www.ctcgrampian.org.uk

National Cycle Network
Sustrans was founded in 1977, to help people travel in ways that benefit their health and the environment. The first officially marked cycle route was the Bristol and Bath Railway Path, a 17-mile traffic-free trail along a disused line. The National Network was officially created in 1995 with a grant from the newly created National Lottery. Spanning the UK, and passing within one mile of 57% of the population, the Network consists of over 13,000 miles of marked walking and cycling routes.

Information about the cycling network, including maps, can be obtained from the cycle network website.
www.sustrans.org.uk

Doonies Farm
Doonies Rare Breeds Farm covers 134 acres on the southern side of Aberdeen from Nigg Bay to Cove.
www.dooniesfarm.co.uk

Kincorth Hill Local Nature Reserve
Kincorth Hill is located on the south side of the city, near the suburb of Kincorth. There are access points from car parks at Abbotswell Crescent and Nigg Way, and from various points along the edge of the Kincorth housing estate.

There is a series of public paths that run across the hillside, through coniferous and deciduous woodland, grassland and heath. The area is excellent for bird-watching or for strolling in a peaceful setting. There is an active ranger service, with local rangers providing tours and talks about the area.

Information about the nature reserve and about the ranger service can be found on the Aberdeen City Council website.
www.aberdeencity.gov.uk

DEE AND DON INSPIRATION

The name Aberdeen can be translated as meaning 'between two rivers', the Dee and the Don. Indeed, the city is dominated by water, not only the coastline with the North Sea, but equally by the water that flows from the Highlands. William Forsyth, a Scottish writer, wrote about Aberdeen:

Thy white foot rests on golden sands;
A radiant robe encircles thee

Of wooded hills and garden lands.
I'll lift my cap and sing they praise,

By silent Don and crystal Dee;
Oh, bravely gentle all thy days,

Fair city by the sea.

No visit to Aberdeen is complete without experiencing a little of the culture, history and the sheer beauty that is on offer from the two very different rivers that have shaped the city. Separated only by a mile of golden sands, the mouths of the rivers look very different. The River Don flows gently through the silt-deposited Donmouth Local Nature Reserve. The waters of the River Dee combine with those of Aberdeen Harbour, majestically creating a water system that is internationally recognised as the hub of the oil and gas industry in the North Sea.

The River Dee

The River Dee starts its 85-mile journey from within the Cairngorms National Park, west of the city. This mountainous place of unique aesthetic and scientific interest, and one of the most extensive of British national parks, consists of over 1,500 square miles of land. The area is rich in wildlife and includes a quarter of Britain's vulnerable plants, birds and animals.

The waters of the River Dee rise upwards on the plateau of Braeriach, Britain's third-highest mountain, from beneath a mossy embankment known as the Wells of Dee. At just over 3,900 feet, the river has the highest source of any in the British Isles.

Gathering pace from its humble beginnings on the Cairngorm massif, the youthful river plunges 500 feet over a cliff edge on the An Garbh Choire (a corrie). The water then combines with the Geldie Burn before emerging into the Linn of Dee, one of Scotland's most visited places of scenic beauty.

Balmoral

Apart from the picturesque nature of the Dee Valley, another reason why the area is important to tourists is because of the

Crystal-clear waters of the Dee, near its source

connections with the Royal Family. Queen Victoria purchased Balmoral Castle in 1848, although the original 'house' was demolished and rebuilt in 1856. Designed by Aberdeen architect William Smith, the castle is a great example of Scots Baronial style, and is now classified by Historic Scotland as a Category A listed building.

The Balmoral Estate, added to by consecutive members of the Royal Family, now covers an area of almost 50,000 acres. As well as its diverse wildlife, forestry, and salmon fishing on the River Dee, the estate contains ancient Caledonian woodland. In her journals, Queen Victoria referred to her Scottish holiday estate as "My dear paradise in the Highlands".

Balmoral sits almost equidistant between two villages on Deeside, Braemar and Ballater. Furthest west is Braemar, where the river meanders majestically through valleys cut millions of years ago by advancing glaciers. The most inhabited area on the upper reaches of the River Dee, Braemar sits at just over 1,100 feet above sea level. Summer temperatures can soar into the low 30s but in the winter temperatures can plummet well into the minus 20s.

The medieval village of Ballater, which formed part of the estates of the Knights of St John in the early 14th century, did not develop significantly until the arrival

of the railway from Aberdeen in 1866. The railway brought tourism to Deeside, with many people keen to catch a glimpse of the royals. The Royal Family visited the village frequently and many of the shops had Royal Warrants bestowed upon them. Today, Ballater is still a thriving tourist attraction, with many people travelling the short journey from Aberdeen to soak up the Highland air and to enjoy the royal heritage that shaped the village.

Mystery and mythology

Of course, it is not only history that intrigues the present-day visitor to Deeside. The area is steeped in mythological mystery, with tales of the supernatural and, quite frankly, bizarre, that lure many people to visit the numerous castles and stately homes. Michael Pegler, in his book *Dee and Don – Inspiration* reflects "There are many tales regarding feuds between the families whose estates span Deeside. One example involves Alexander Gordon, known as Black Alister, and Arthur Forbes, known as Black Airter.

"Alister supported the expulsion of the French in 1560 and became an earnest supporter of Mary Queen of Scots following the clemency she afforded him. Alister also succeeded in resisting the plunder of Deeside by the Mackintoshes, a clan intent on taking the fertile Deeside land for themselves. The invaders

The River Dee at Braemar

butchered Alister's kin, the Gordons of Knock.

"However, surprisingly in this rampant butchering of Alister's kin, one local man, the Laird of Strathgirnock, known as Black Airter, was left unharmed. This smelled of treachery to the Gordons, an action worthy of reprisal. They [Black Alister and his men] burned Airter's home while he was away.

"Incredibly, peace was restored – for a time. But events took a strange twist some years later. A loving liaison occurred between Francis Gordon, the son of the Laird of Knock, and Black Airter's daughter. Francis Gordon requested a 'thigging', an engagement present from his prospective father-in-law. For some reason, probably deep-seated resentment, Airter struck him with his sword, thinking that it was still sheathed securely. However, as the scabbard came loose from its sheath so did Francis' head!

"After this mishap, Airter went into hiding while Alister took possession of Airter's estate at Strathgirnock. But Airter returned with help and surprised Alister's seven sons while they cut peat on Airter's former land. Airter proceeded to butcher them all. He must have taken great pride in his gruesome task, for he went to the trouble of exhibiting each head impaled upon a spade. When Alister heard the news, the shock caused him to fall from the staircase of his castle to his death."

Lochnagar

A few miles east of the present-day village of Strathgirnock lies the road to Glen Muick, which leads to the car park of one of the most inspiring mountains in the north-east of Scotland – Lochnagar. Along both the North Deeside Road and the South Deeside Road from Aberdeen, there are numerous coffee shops, art galleries and studios, all with one thing in common. Wherever you go, you are sure to find a painting of that iconic north-east mountain.

Lochnagar, with its three peaks, curves around a massive corrie that encloses a beautiful loch by the same name, Loch Nagar. Cac Carn Beag, at just under 3,800 feet, is the highest summit and lies to the north-west of the massif.

Located on the royal estate of Balmoral, popular with the current Royal Family, Lochnagar was a favourite of Queen Victoria, who often explored the many paths and trails in the area. Even today, the royals love to explore the heather-clad hills and summits around the Balmoral Estate. The mountain is the setting for the children's story *The Old Man of Lochnagar*, written by Prince Charles and published in 1980.

The mountain and surrounding countryside inspired one of Britain's greatest poets, George Gordon Byron. Known today as Lord Byron, he wrote, amongst other poems, the classic *Don Juan*. Inspired by his short time living in Deeside, Byron penned the beautiful poem *Dark Lochnagar*, which was later set to music by the Scottish folk group, the Corries.

Kevin Massie, a Scottish writer and mountaineer, reflects "Lochnagar is a great mountain, possibly the finest in the whole of the Cairngorms range. Not the highest, but certainly the most spectacular, with the impressive corrie, and great view from the accessible summit.

"I think it is the ever-changing atmosphere that appeals to most people. No two trips up the mountain will be the same. One day the granite top will sparkle in the sunshine whereas another day will bring dark moody shadows cast by the sun's low angle.

"Walking up to the summit when the sky is cloudy seems to bring out the beauty of the openness of this area of Scotland. The plateau is massive, open and barren. It is quite awesome when standing at the top, particularly when there is no one else there.

Glen Muick is another great place to visit. Even if there is no intention of walking right to the top of Lochnagar, a gentle stroll around the loch can be really enjoyable and spectacular."

So, Deeside offers an abundance of beauty, history and tales of the past. But Donside, a little way to the north of the Dee valley, offers much as well. A local verse sums up the relationship between the two valleys:

A mile of the Don's worth twa o' the Dee,
Except it be for fish an' tree.

In other words, Deeside has the finer fishing and forests, but Donside has the best farmland, with some excellent trout fishing as well.

The River Don

The embryonic River Don comes into being on the Ladder Hills, a ridge of rolling uplands, as a confluence of several streams including the Feith Bhait, Meoir Veannaich and the Allt nan Aighean. The summits of the Ladder Hills, at around 2,500 feet, are collectively classed as a Site of Special Scientific Interest. The golden plover, dunlin, dotterel and raven can be found flying around the hilltops, as well as the hen harrier and golden eagle. Large populations of red grouse, red deer and the mountain hare live on the hillsides.

enjoy a gentle walk around
Loch Muick or venture up
onto the magnificent
plateau of Lochnagar

journey around the many
castles and other ancient
buildings that line
the Dee and Don

visit the Cairngorm
National Park and enjoy
numerous leisure and
sporting opportunities

explore old and
new at the Grampian
Transport Museum,
Alford

Highlights

Gathering pace as it travels, the river runs through the parish of Strathdon, with the impressive Lonach Hill towering over the area. On the fourth Saturday of August each year the hill takes on a special attraction within this unique area of Aberdeenshire.

Formed in 1823 by Sir Charles Forbes, 1st Baronet of Newe and Edinglassie, the Lonach Highlanders belong to the Lonach Highland and Friendly Society. Drawn from inhabitants of Strathdon, the society aims to fulfil the original mission set up over 180 years ago, to "preserve Highland dress, the Gaelic tongue, and supporting loyal, peaceful, and manly conduct, and the promotion of social and benevolent feelings among the inhabitants of the district".

The Highlanders parade during the annual Lonach Highland Games to officially open them. Tradition has it that along the route of the march from Bellabeg to Strathdon, the column stops for a 'wee dram'. Led by the patron of the society, Chief of the Forbes clan, the Highlanders march proudly alongside the pipes and drums of the Lonach Band to their meeting place at the bottom of the hill.

South-west from Strathdon, where the Tornahaish Burn meets with the River Don, is the village of Tornahaish, where there is a Roman Catholic Chapel dated

1880. Michael Pegler, in *Dee and Don – Inspiration,* reflects "Not too far from here the work of stone dykers unearthed a cache of silver coins in 1822,

"The coins were found on the western side of a hill, near a place called Tom Fuaraich. The majority of coins were from the reign of Henry III, with some from the reign of William the Lion, and two were from King John's time.

"There were two rings among the treasure; one was iron gilt mounted with a pale sapphire. Coincidentally, in 1829 a similar ring was found in the Bishop of Chichester's coffin, circa 1146.

"Another great piece from history is the Migvie Stone, which has a Pictish antecedence from the ninth century. The stone is located in the churchyard within the remnants of Migvie Castle. Standing over six feet tall, the face of the stone is occupied by a carved cross filled with knotwork decoration."

A few miles east of Migvie is the village of Tillyfour. Although it is picturesque and has a good pedigree in its own right, Tillyfour is most famous for one of its residents. William McCombie, born in 1805, was known as the King of Grazers for his ground-breaking work in developing the now world-famous breed of Aberdeen Angus cattle.

Corgarff Castle

A farmer's son, McCombie passed over a university education at Aberdeen to concentrate on cultivating his father's fields. Becoming a cattle dealer at first and tenant farmer in 1829, he then moved onto breeding cattle. He was awarded many prizes including the highest prize in his specialism, first at the Paris Exposition of 1878.

A famous specimen of McCombie's endeavours, Black Prince, won several awards in 1867. The cattle even came to the notice of Queen Victoria, who enjoyed its beef as a Christmas gift from the farmer. The Queen visited McCombie at Tillyfour some years later. McCombie became the first tenant farmer elected to the House of Commons in 1868. He died at his home in 1880, and a statue to commemorate his great work was unveiled in the village by Charles, Prince of Wales, in the presence of Queen Elizabeth, the Queen Mother, in 2001.

As the river progresses towards the North Sea, it passes through Inverurie, about 17 miles from the city. Home of the Gordons, Inverurie was given a charter in 1558. However, it is more famous for the establishment of the Aberdonian Canal at Port Elphinstone. Opened in 1805, the canal linked the village with the city of Aberdeen. However, with the advent of rail, the canal only survived a few years and closed in 1854. The name, Port Elphinstone, still exists today and is

something of an anomaly in the farming-rich countryside that surrounds the small village.

As the journeys end for both rivers, their geographies are now quite different.

From a simple 'river mouth', the Dee was opened to form a harbour. During the 18th and 19th centuries, the North Pier was developed and a new channel created between 1869 and 1873, which facilitated the reclamation of an improved harbour.

A picture of the Dee estuary from previous centuries would reveal a narrow channel blocked by banks of sand and an enormous rock called the Knock Metellan. Cleverly, this rock was attached to a ring of empty barrels so that it could be towed away, thus opening the channel.

The 1850s witnessed trade, beginning with the Chinese tea markets where clippers sailed for China from Aberdeen. Routes to Australia and South Africa quickly followed and shipbuilding in the harbour took off, with 3,000 ships being launched from Aberdeen over two centuries.

The harbour in Aberdeen is now home to the hundreds of vessels that support the oil and gas industry in the North Sea. The Aberdeen Harbour Board, which administers the harbour, maintains and improves 350 acres of land and water,

Mar Lodge Estate

four miles of quays, 20 deep-water berths, with accommodation for handling over five million tonnes of cargo every year.

The final reaches of the River Don are a little different from those of the more illustrious Dee. The river flows through Woodside, once home of cloth-weaving, paper-making and other industries. However, the Don, as it flows to the North Sea, passes through a magnificent local nature reserve. Groups of bottlenose dolphins are often seen at the entrance to the River Don, together with porpoises and seals.

Only a mile of golden sand separates the Dee and Don estuaries. Standing on the beach looking westward, it is difficult to believe that those rivers have incredibly different journeys. But those journeys have helped to shape the city.

To explore the culture of Aberdeen, much can be sought locally. However, to truly appreciate how such a city has been influenced over the years by royalty, by great achievements in farming and by war and conflict, the journey of exploration should extend outwards a little. A trip along the North Deeside Road to Ballater and Braemar to experience beauty and heritage, together with a short journey along Donside to Strathdon, is surely needed to complete the exploration experience.

Bridge of Don

Exploring

The Deeside

The A93 road, which leaves Aberdeen on the west of the city near to Great Western Road, runs parallel with the River Dee right to the village of Braemar. From the city centre to Braemar the route is a little over 58 miles. The road can be busy with tourist coaches, particularly during summer months. There are many small villages en route along the A93, together with numerous coffee shops, art galleries and other attractions. A great place to stop for a short break is Crathes Castle, about 16 miles from the city. Turrets, towers and gargoyles, winding staircases, ornate ceilings and ancient yew trees combine to make one of Scotland's most popular attractions a worthwhile visit.

More information about Crathes Castle can be found on the National Trust for Scotland website.
www.nts.org.uk

Ballater

Forty miles from Aberdeen, on the A93, is the small town of Ballater. Famous for its royal connections and the restored railway station, Ballater is the gateway to the Cairngorms. A little further along the main road leads to spectacular walks, while over the bridge, on the B976, the narrow road leads up Glen Muick to Loch Muick and to the start of the trails on Lochnagar.

Balmoral Castle and Estate

Set amongst magnificent scenery in the shadow of Lochnagar, the Balmoral Estate covers about 50,000 acres of heather-clad hills, ancient Caledonian woodland and large stretches of the River Dee. The grounds and gardens of the castle are open on a daily basis throughout the summer months. It is always best to check out the website, because restrictions may apply when members of the Royal Family are in residence.
www.balmoralcastle.com

Braemar

Walk in the Highlands of Scotland, spend a day visiting local art galleries, take part in the Whisky Trail, or take a wildlife safari around the hills – all of those are possible from Braemar. Set at an altitude of 1,100 feet above sea level, this picturesque village marks the end of the Deeside road. Just before entering the village, the A93 forks left to Blairgowrie and Tayside. The right fork leads to the village. On the west side of Braemar, the main road carries on towards the Linn of Dee, which is truly the road-end. The rushing water and the ancient bridge over the River Dee are definitely worth exploring, before returning to the village for a well-deserved afternoon tea in one of the two famous hotels, the Fife Arms and the Invercauld.

The following websites provide further information about the area.
www.visitcairngorms.com
www.fifearmsbraemar.com
www.invercauld.org

Donside

The River Don is equally as impressive as its counterpart to the south. The A944, which leaves Aberdeen via Queens Road, past Hazlehead Park and then via Westhill, passes through many villages as it keeps in line with the river. Alford, 25 miles west of Aberdeen, with its massive camping site and recreational park, is worth a visit. The Grampian Transport Museum is a must while passing through Alford. The museum boasts an amazing range of transport exhibits, from travelling chariots of the 1800s, to some of the fastest cars ever made. Many exhibits are 'climb aboard' and hands-on.

Check out the Grampian Transport Museum website for more information about opening times and events.
www.gtm.org.uk

Strathdon

Further west on the A944 is Strathdon. This place is actually classed as an "informal geographical area", meaning that there are no precise boundaries of where it begins or ends. Home to the Lonach Highland Gathering, Strathdon is a collection of communities and hamlets, spread across a wide section of the main road.

For more information about the Lonach Highland Gathering, visit their website.
www.lonach.org

The main road joins the A939, an old military road, near to the village of Corgarff. From there, a very steep climb leads to the Lecht centre, where it is possible to ski in winter and have fun on the hillside with Deval Karts in the summer!
www.lecht.co.uk

Tomintoul

Lying at 1,170 feet above sea level, Tomintoul boasts of being the highest village in the Cairngorms National Park. Being set in such a beautiful location means there is plenty to do – from horse- and pony-trekking to mountain biking or walking – and the village and surrounding area have to be seen to be believed. Tomintoul marks the end of the area known as Donside.

For more information, visit the Tomintoul information website.
www.visittomintoul.co.uk

LITTLE CHELSEA

In 1379, King Robert II, grandson of Robert the Bruce, granted to the "trusty burgesses" and the community of Aberdeen "the whole land of the tenement of Rubbyslaw" that lay next to the burgh and city of Aberdeen. This was an important section of land because it not only provided access to the western part of the city but was also lush land for building upon.

Today, with its exquisite granite buildings and tree-lined terraces, this part of Aberdeen is known as the West End. From those early beginnings, when the land was granted to the new lairds, the West End has retained an exclusive lifestyle, to the extent that it is now dubbed Little Chelsea. Such is the remarkable nature of the city of Aberdeen that within two miles of the city centre small boutiques replace high-street chains and French patisseries replace shopping mall coffee outlets. Even the pace of life seems to slow down in Little Chelsea.

For an annual fee of one silver penny, to be paid into the king's treasury at every Feast of Pentecost (the fiftieth day after Easter Sunday), the land of Rubislaw was granted to the people of Aberdeen. Although it is difficult to detail accurately

the exact boundary of this land in today's geography, the lands of Rubislaw was probably bounded by King's Gate to the north and Great Western Road to the south, and ran from the bottom end of Union Street (Holburn junction) westwards to Kepplestone.

When the Freedom Lands were dispersed in 1551, Rubislaw was feuded to Alexander Rutherford, a prominent citizen of Aberdeen. Rutherford, who was provost of the city eight times between 1591 and 1614, acted as the city's commissioner to the Estates (the Scottish Parliament) on several occasions. He was much in favour of the proposed union between the kingdoms of Scotland and England and he presented a case for union in the presence of King James. Legend has it that the king was so impressed by Rutherford's oration that he drew a diamond ring from his finger and presented it to the provost. In spite of this, the Union of Parliaments did not come about until 1707.

Sir Arthur Forbes acquired Rubislaw after the death of Rutherford. The estate passed to various descendants of the Forbes family until, in 1687, Thomas Forbes sold Rubislaw to one of the most prominent merchants of the day, George Skene.

Following a successful trading career in Danzig, Poland, George Skene returned to his home town of Aberdeen in 1665. A few months after returning to Scotland, Skene bought the Wester Fintray Estate in Aberdeenshire. In 1669 he bought one of the finest and best-known houses in Aberdeen, the handsome Guestrow mansion that now bears his name, Provost Skene's House.

Dating from 1545, Provost Skene's House is a rare example from Aberdeen's medieval burgh architecture. It is thought that Skene commissioned the carved plaster ceilings in the 17th century. An attic gallery, and a Renaissance painted ceiling that includes strapwork decorations and religious scenes, were added later.

Sir George Skene, knighted by the Duke of York, brother of King Charles II, was a bachelor and his estate descended via his grand-nephew and heir to George, fourth Skene of Rubislaw. However, George died at the early age of 40, whereby his elder son, also George, inherited the estate at six years of age. He too died young and the estate passed to his brother, James.

After studying law, James Skene was called to the Scottish Bar in 1797, where he began a friendship with a fellow lawyer, the writer Sir Walter Scott. He and Scott had much in common,

including serving as officers in the Edinburgh Light Horse, formed in 1807 to defend the country against a possible invasion from France. It was during this time, serving in the army, that Sir Walter Scott conceived the idea for his book, *Marmion*, which was published the following year.

Skene lived for many years in Edinburgh and it was from there that inspiration for developing his estate in Aberdeen came. His vision was to create a northern version of Edinburgh's New Town. However, the Rubislaw estate brought many problems to Skene. From disputes over rights of access to the flourishing Rubislaw Quarry (to take stone for public buildings) to the scheme to pipe Denburn water through the estate, these tedious problems dragged on for years.

The arrival of the Skene Turnpike in 1803, a new road that linked the west side of Aberdeen to the parish countryside further west of the city, made the lands of Rubislaw more attractive to purchasers and developers. Skene sold portions of the estate until finally, in 1860, the last of the estate was bought by Sir Alexander Anderson. Fifteen years later, being in financial difficulty, Anderson sold Rubislaw to the City of Aberdeen Land Association.

The birth of the West End of Aberdeen possibly owed much to the Skene Turnpike. The new road was approved by the County of Aberdeen turnpike trustees in 1800. Hard to believe it now, but nothing of Queen's Cross and Albyn Place, which link Rubislaw to Union Street and the city centre, existed at the time of the turnpike's creation. Green fields and open country with a few hamlets were all that were there. In spite of disagreements between councillors and businessmen, the new road was opened by 1803, with the first tollhouse, albeit only a wooden hut on Carden Place, taking fees from travellers.

"Albyn Place and Rubislaw Terrace are stars in the crown of the West End," comments Diane Morgan in her book *Lost Aberdeen, the Freedom Lands*. Diane continues "Albyn Place fared very well. It had taken over from the pocket estate as the place to live, being almost as prestigious, easier to run, handy for town, with ample room for servants, horses, gigs, staff quarters and landscaped gardens. By the 1880s the array of top people living there (Albyn Place) was utterly formidable." Those 'formidable' people included an admiral at No.3; Francis Edmond, the lawyer and Free Kirk stalwart, at No.5; Theodore Crombie of Grandholm at No.18; and Alexander Rose

of Donaldson Rose, ship-owners, timber merchants and lairds of Hazlehead, at No.42.

Another famous resident of the area was George Washington Wilson, a local and well-known photographer, who staked his claim to be a member of the new West End society. Although his studio and home in Crown Street, in the city centre of Aberdeen, were more than adequate, even for the 'photographer of the Queen', perhaps he felt that a more salubrious address was needed. He occupied No.1 Queen's Cross.

Queen's Cross remained a semi-circle of beautiful granite houses until, in 1874, Rubislaw Parish Church appeared. George Washington Wilson had appointed himself unofficial conservator of Queen's Cross and the church's arrival caused him some concern. He felt that only Aberdeen granite was good enough for buildings within the area but he became aware of the plan to build the new church from sandstone. Alas, it was too late for him to change the construction method but he put measures in place to ensure that no other building would be built in Queen's Cross from anything other than granite.

Queen's Cross was fast becoming a centre of innovation. In her book, Diane Morgan comments "George Washington Wilson's townhouse boasted Aberdeen's first domestic central-heating system and plate-glass windows. Rubislaw was the first established church in Aberdeen to have a pipe organ. No one local knew how to play it, so Miss Lucas, a sprightly London lady of Italian descent and 'a skilled harpist', was brought to Aberdeen and played the organ successfully for many years. Vast crowds journeyed out to Queen's Cross to hear her at the keyboards as well, presumably, as the Reverend Professor Henry Cowan DD in the pulpit.

"A lively correspondence ensued in the local press between those who angrily maintained that the introduction of a 'kist o' whistles' into a Presbyterian service was backsliding into Popery and those who supported the innovation on musical grounds.

"Satan, as usual, was lurking nearby in the form of an entrepreneurial Aberdeen lawyer, John Watt, who built an innova- tory leisure centre alongside Rubislaw Church in 1877. It had a cement-floored roller-skating circuit laid out around central flower-beds. A band played in the gallery of the main building, and at night the ground was lit up by fairy lamps. A croquet lawn, bowling green, a tennis ground and an American-style skittle alley were to the rear, along Queen's Lane North."

Innovation did not end with cutting-edge buildings and amenities. In 1874, Aberdeen District Tramways recognised a need to transport people from the newly formed West End to the city centre. The company started a service, with a frequency of every ten minutes, between Queen's Cross and the North Church in Queen Street (Queen Street is not near to Queen's Cross; it is right in the heart of the city). Queen's Cross became the main horse-tram depot, with the superintendent's office being located there too.

A quirky area within the city

The affluence that prevailed in this area of Aberdeen has continued to this day. Although many of the privately owned homes are now owned by firms of accountants, lawyers, oil companies and consultancies, the area has managed to maintain something different. Neil Massie, owner of the coffee shop Rocksalt and Snails, comments "Aberdeen, unlike many other cities, doesn't have lots of different and individual centres. For example, you can go to Edinburgh and you've got Stockbridge, Morningside, the Grassmarket, all with their own unique communities and identities. Aberdeen lacks that in many ways because the focus has always been on Union Street, as a shopping hub.

St Mary Episcopal Church, Carden Place

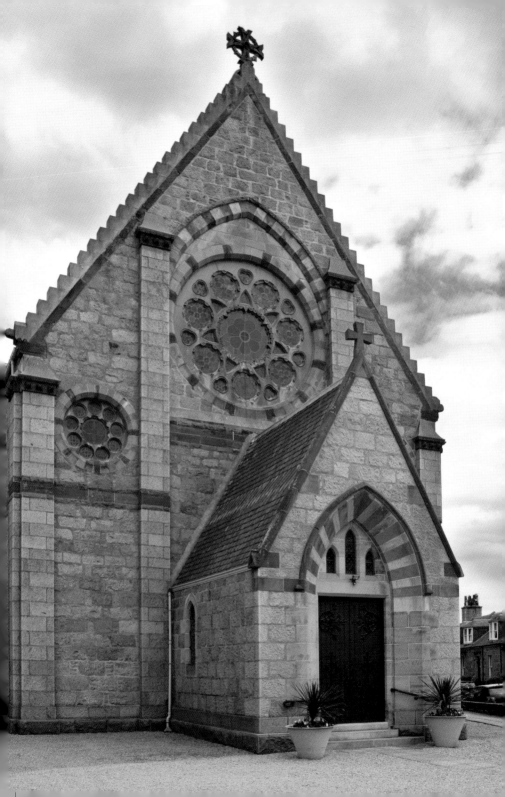

"This little area of Aberdeen does have its own identity. Although this is an affluent part of the city, with many people working in the centre of town, this Little Chelsea is known for providing 'something different'. There are some great boutiques, with brands of clothes that you wouldn't find anywhere else in Aberdeen, or even in Scotland. There are fantastic art galleries, antique dealers and, of course, wonderful places to eat.

"Aberdeen is truly a cosmopolitan city and no more so than in this part of town. We get lots of people visiting Little Chelsea, including Russians, French, South Americans, Americans and Germans. We are getting a nice continental feel to this part of the city."

Incidentally, this deli-café, which is in St Swithin Street, just off Queen's Cross, takes its name from the Shetland rock band Rocksalt and Nails. Neil remarks "I was heading to a friend's barbeque one evening when I heard Rocksalt and Nails on the car radio, and it was an epiphany at the moment, it was great. Nails became Snails, and the deli opened!"

Quirkiness and innovation are synony-mous with Little Chelsea. Few high-street shops can boast that their customers are greeted with a cup of coffee before they browse for frocks and other clothing. Even

fewer high-street shops keep a diary of a customer's purchases, so that no other customer buys the same outfit. Andrea Brodie, owner of Frox on Thistle Street, is certainly no stranger to providing the personal touch. "We are unique in what we do here in Aberdeen," says Andrea. "Not only do we specialise in dresses for cocktail parties, cruises, school proms and black-tie functions, but we also ensure that no two of our dresses go to the same function.

"The idea for keeping a customer diary started when I worked in retail on the high street. Many times I heard customers getting stressed about whether a similar dress would be worn by another person. There is nothing worse for a lady than turning up to an occasion and finding someone else wearing a similar outfit. So, we ask people what they want, and we ask where they are going. We try really hard to keep records so that we never create a clash at a function.

"This part of Aberdeen lends itself to being different and to offering a little more time for customers. In this area – Little Chelsea – the shops are smaller and much more personal than in some other areas of the city. That means we can be different and, more importantly, we can offer a more personal service. People love to be looked after and they are very

have a break from
exploring at
Rock Salt and Snails

find quirky shops
with quirky names
in Little Chelsea

stroll through
the gardens and stop
for a picnic lunch

GALLERY HEINZEL
CONTEMPORARY ART

visit the gallery
to view the best
of Aberdeen's
contemporary artists

Highlights

impressed by our diary concept. Not only does it provide some confidence to people that they will have a unique frock, but it also offers the opportunity to get to know our customers, which is really important in this part of town.

"I love working in Little Chelsea because we get many local customers but we also get many visitors. People visit this part of town because they want to find something a little more unusual than they might in the shopping centres. I would say to any visitor to Aberdeen, take a little time out and visit this great part of the city."

From the wonderful history and geography to the warm hospitality offered by the numerous small shops, boutiques and eateries, Little Chelsea does indeed have something unique to offer the visitor. From the early beginnings of this part of Aberdeen to its present-day culture, the West End has been able to retain its exclusivity and charm, to delight those who seek something different. A day spent walking around this area and browsing the shops is a definite must.

Exploring

Provost Skene's House

Dating from 1545, Provost Skene's House now showcases an attractive series of period rooms, furnished to show how people lived in the 17th, 18th and early 19th centuries. The house was named after one of Aberdeen's most famous residents, Lord Provost George Skene, who is thought to have commissioned the wonderfully carved plaster ceilings.

Open Mondays to Saturdays, Provost Skene's House is located at Guestrow, between Broad Street and Flourmill Lane.
www.aagm.co.uk

Rubislaw and Queens Terrace Gardens

Although these are classed as two separate public gardens, they are bisected only by a minor road running between them so they can be classed as one park. There is a fountain made from pink granite in the middle of this small picturesque park, and the trees that line the rectangular park are over 100 years old.

Right in the heart of Little Chelsea, Rubislaw and Queens Terrace Gardens make a nice link between the shops of Thistle Street (at the Holburn end of Union Street) and those of Queen's Cross and St Swithin Street. A stroll through the park on a nice day, with perhaps a picnic lunch from the many fine patisseries on Thistle Street, is a great way to absorb the culture of this unique area of Aberdeen.

Rubislaw Parish Church

Rubislaw Church was built in 1875 and stands at the heart of the West End of Aberdeen. The church enjoys a long-standing tradition of choral, organ and instrumental music during Sunday worship. The choir has a varied repertoire, from 16th-century to 21st-century music, while instruments such as violins, violas, cellos, French horns and flutes add to the magnificent organ music within the church.

For details of services and musical recitals, visit the church website.
www.rubislawchurch.org.uk

Queen's Cross Parish Church

On 18 April 1881, the first morning service at Queen's Cross Parish Church was taken by the Rev Walter Smith, whose hymn *Immortal, invisible, God only Wise* is still a favourite in the church today. This is another fine example of a 19th-century building that was constructed in the West End to meet the needs of the growing population of that area of the city.

Details of services can be found on the church website.
www.queenscrosschurch.org.uk

Rocksalt and Snails
Just minutes from the heart of the city, this exquisite coffee shop is a sanctuary nestled in Little Chelsea where one can take a break from the history to enjoy a coffee and delightful treats.

Open seven days a week, the coffee shop is at 40 St Swithin Street.
www.rocksaltandsnails.co.uk

Frox
Whether to browse for that next little black number, or simply to enjoy the hospitality and personal service of this area of Aberdeen, a visit to Frox is a must.

Frox is at 28 Thistle Street.
www.frox.uk.com

Some other highlights
La Gourmandise, a traditional French patisserie first started in Aberdeen 20 years ago, is at 63 Thistle Street.
www.lagourmandise.co.uk

From candles to glassware, Nova Gifts, at 18 Chapel Street, has a wide range of unique items.
www.novagifts.co.uk

Gallery Heinzel specialises in Scottish contemporary art at 24 Thistle Street.
www.galleryheinzel.com

Period jewellery, silver, ceramics, crystal and brassware can all be found at the interesting Elizabeth Watt antique shop at 69 Thistle Street.
www.elizabethwattrestoration.co.uk

If you are in need of a manicure, pop into the Express Nail Bar at 39 St Swithin Street.
www.thenailroomtoo.co.uk

The Light of Bengal restaurant, 13 Rose Street, established in Aberdeen since 1978, is a favourite with locals and visitors to the city.
www.lightofbengal.com

Established in 2001, Rustico is a friendly and family-run Mediterranean restaurant at 62 Union Row.
www.rustico-restaurant.co.uk

141

AFTERNOON TEA
IN THE MERCHANT QUARTER

The official website of Aberdeen's Merchant Quarter says that it is the "beat and the soul" of the city. Catering for visitors and locals, this small and compact part of the city, which is rich in history and architecture, now boasts an eclectic mix of independent businesses, restaurants, bars, shopping and entertainment.

Sandwiched between two major shopping areas of Aberdeen – Union Square to the south and Union Street with the Bon Accord and St Nicholas Shopping Centres to the north – the Merchant Quarter truly is unique within the city. Once home to merchant trading companies, because of its close proximity to the harbour, the area has been rejuvenated into a vibrant and cheerful contemporary district, with boutiques and hotels occupying premises once used to import and export goods around the world. There is nothing better than sitting in the Carmelite enjoying the quintessentially British pastime of 'afternoon tea' while reflecting on the history of this charming district of Aberdeen.

The name Carmelite comes from early settlers in this area of Scotland. Historical records indicate that the Carmelite friars originated from a small group of hermits who, after travelling on a pilgrimage to Palestine from Europe, settled on Mount Carmel. In 1226, Pope Honorius III granted approval to the friars and the Order grew rapidly. By 1242 they had entered England and, such were their numbers, three years later they held their first 'general chapter' where St Simon Stock was elected to General of the Order.

The Carmelites arrived in Aberdeen in 1273. Occupying part of the area now known as the Green, the friars quickly established their community. Although not large in numbers, probably only six friars, they built up close connections with townspeople, resulting in people leaving money and personal belongings to the Order.

In 1994 a construction company, planning to build new houses in the Green, instigated a major archaeological project that revealed how the Carmelites may have built their structures. Alison Cameron, an archaeologist with Aberdeen City Council at the time of the dig, comments "When the friars originally set up their church they probably did so

with wood and then they would have built a stone church and other stone buildings. We found lines of post holes parallel to the stone church so we think that a wooden structure would have been built first, allowing the friars to start preaching their cause to the locals.

"We found a lot of burials when we carried out the excavations. It would have been very prestigious for local people to be buried within a friary church. People would have paid for their remains to be buried by the friars. Over 200 burials, most of them in the west end of the church, were found.

"The human remains we found were quite indicative of life during medieval Scotland. We found lots of evidence of disease and injuries on the skeletons and quite a few severe head injuries, possibly caused by sword wounds."

Although life during medieval Scotland would have been very different from life today, the Carmelites were quite advanced for the period. Alison says "Lead pipes and copper alloy taps were found when we excavated the site. We know that the Green had a well, so finding the pipes led us to believe the Carmelites of the 13th century had a well-developed plumbing system, the earliest known in Aberdeen.

"Our excavations found hundreds of pieces of window glass, roof slates and floor tiles. None of those were actually in place when we found them, probably because they had been stripped off the roofs during the Reformation period. We did find evidence of scaffolding and pulleys, indicating that the Carmelites were very sophisticated by that period."

The site of the archaeological dig has been built over today, but thousands of artifacts from the excavation were collected and are now stored by Aberdeen City Council.

There was another friary close to the Carmelites in the Green. The Order of the Holy Trinity (or Trinitarians), founded in France at the end of the 12th century, existed for the primary task of raising money to pay ransoms that were demanded on Christians taken hostage during their pilgrimages to the Holy Land. Similar to their neighbouring friars, the Trinitarians forged close relationships with prominent local families, resulting in them becoming a rich institution within the city.

The Reformation reached Aberdeen in January 1560. Although believed to be a relatively peaceful occurrence in the city, many churches and friaries were destroyed

browse the shops
in the Union Square
Shopping Centre

sample Scottish Whisky in
the numerous pubs around
the Merchant Quarter

enjoy afternoon 'tea'
at the Carmelite

sit back and soak up
the atmosphere in
this historic, and
now contemporary,
part of the city

Highlights

during this period. However, although the Trinitarians vacated their buildings during the Reformation, most of the structures remained intact. Following the Reformation the buildings were used for a number of different purposes until, in 1631, the buildings were sold to William Guild who then made them over to the Incorporated Trades.

Crafts and tradesmen

Craftsmen of Aberdeen belonged to one of seven separate guilds. These were the weavers, bakers, tailors, hammermen, shoemakers, wrights & coopers, and fleshers. In 1222, Alexander II granted Aberdeen a charter that confirmed the existence of a merchant guild, the weavers, with the monopoly for making cloth. Other guilds were formed over the following 300 years, with the most recent, the fleshers, being founded in 1534. When Dr Guild gifted the Trinity Monastery to the Trades in the 17th century no mention was made of the fleshers in the deed of gift but, in 1657, a special agreement was made by Dr Guild that the fleshers should be allowed to join the Trades, who had a common meeting house and hospital (a retirement place) on the site of the Trinitarians.

The Trades moved to new premises, on Union Street, in 1846. The old buildings of the Trinitarians were demolished in the 19th century when the railway came to Aberdeen. New streets were formed, Exchange Street and Guild Street, which still exist today.

Around about the same time that the railway came to Aberdeen, a new market building was constructed in the Green. Markets had been held in this area for many years, but the new building provided cover for the numerous farmers from surrounding areas to sell their goods. Designed by Archibald Simpson, and completed in 1842, the market was over 100-feet long. Suffering a major fire some years later, the market was rebuilt in 1882 and demolished in the 1970s to make room for what is now the current market.

"There is nowhere in Aberdeen with as much atmosphere as the market in the Green," says Peter Ferguson, owner of one of the shops within the new market. "There is a very long tradition of market trading in the Green. People come from all around the north-east of Scotland to buy fresh products and fish. Locals and tourists alike enjoy the very 'local' atmosphere that exists within this area of the city. Outside, there are often stalls and inside you can buy a wide range of things, from food to clothing and craft products. You can even have a cup of tea and a buttery."

The Green, once home to the Carmelites

Also known as a 'rowie', the Aberdeen buttery is almost like a flattened croissant, but more salty. Noted for their flaky texture and buttery taste, they are often eaten toasted with butter and jam. Their high fat content makes them very hot when toasted. It is believed that this savoury Scottish roll has its origins in the late 19th century when Aberdeen fishermen ate them; the high fat content meant that the rolls could keep longer when at sea.

Commerce and trading

Aberdeen's shipping industry, although very prosperous, had a dark side too, which was associated with the Green. A stone-built house near to the steps that lead from the Green to Union Street was reportedly once used to house kidnapped children who were awaiting shipment to America.

Britain's American colonies were desperate for labour in the early part of the 18th century. Several Aberdeen merchants established a slave trade to America, kidnapping local children and sending them off to work in the US. Once kidnapped, children were held in a variety of locations around Aberdeen, one of which was 'the barn' in the Green. The most famous of the children shipped off to America was Peter Williamson, known as Indian Peter. After returning to Britain

he wrote a book about his experiences in the States.

Another remarkable story associated with the Green is that of the Catholic Apostolic Church, a building built for worship, later used as a banana-ripening warehouse, and finally as a café today. Built in 1880 and used by a church movement that preached the imminence of the second coming of Christ, the congregation rapidly diminished during the early 20th century. The church congregation moved to other premises and the building was taken over by Knowles, the fruit and vegetable wholesaler.

Formed in 1886 by Charles Knowles, the fruit grower had orchards in Kent and Dublin. The company started a wholesale operation in Aberdeen in 1929, establishing themselves as the largest importer of green bananas in the north-east of Scotland. After many years of supplying the royal household with fruit and vegetables, Knowles was awarded the first of its Royal Warrants in 1972.

Joining the company in 1968, the present managing director, Ian Cowie, took over Knowles at the height of the oil industry boom in the city. The company became the only direct supplier of fruit and vegetables to oil rigs in the North Sea. Café Musa now occupies the building.

Hub of central Aberdeen

"Musa is a restaurant, art gallery and live music venue in the Merchant Quarter of Aberdeen," mentions their website. "It is a haven from conformity and the mundane, where fresh, contemporary food lives alongside cutting-edge art and live music against the canvas of a 19th-century church." Those words very much sum-up the new Green. From the early beginnings of the area in the 13th century to the present-day quirkiness of this part of the city, the Merchant Quarter is contemporary yet still seems to retain an atmosphere from the past.

The official website of the Merchant Quarter lists 14 places for food and drink. Ranging from the 'traditional' Scottish atmosphere of a local pub to the more contemporary Bistro Verde, this small area of Aberdeen really does have cuisine to suit all tastes. Of Bistro Verde, a local journalist wrote in the *Aberdeen Evening Express* "From cod and haddock to tuna and halibut, the menu at this cosy-but-classy joint is almost as diverse as the ocean itself. It's lovely to have such a varied choice, which included a vast specials board, but for someone as indecisive as me it meant an extra 10 minutes of humming and hawing before finally making my choice."

It is not only cuisine that is on offer in the Merchant Quarter. There are nine shops, three hotels and a few other attractions within the area. One attraction that is being promoted is the Whisky Walk, which features 12 locations in the Merchant Quarter – all within walking distance – where the famous Scottish drink can be sampled.

Conveniently, there is a bus that runs from Aberdeen Bus Station to the Glen Garioch Distillery, one of the featured distilleries on the Whisky Walk. The Glen Garioch Distillery is one of Scotland's oldest, founded in 1797. Highland-region whiskies are distinctive from their Islay and Lowland counterparts, the former being more peaty while the latter are light in colour. The Highlands are home to an eclectic group of distillers, which means much more variety in their product.

If at the end of the Whisky Walk a much-needed rest is the priority, the Merchant Quarter has taken care of that too. There are three hotels within this small geographic area. The Douglas Hotel, built at the height of the Victorian era, has been welcoming guests since 1848, while the 32-bedroom Sopranos is a "little turreted extravaganza", an architectural miniature of baronial and gothic design. Alternatively, there is the Carmelite where pampering is taken to a new level. Indulgence, comfort and a hearty welcome all await you at this quirky hotel.

Here you can enjoy an "intoxicating afternoon tea" that consists of a selection of cocktails served from vintage china teapots, along with traditional sandwiches, scones, cakes and strawberries. Traditional leaf tea can also be served!

When the Carmelite friars built their first wooden structures as a centre for preaching the word of God, little would they have known their influence would live for centuries. To this day, the Merchant Quarter is different, just as in the 13th century when the friars would probably have been seen as slightly out of the ordinary. Quirky, different, contemporary, unusual, eccentric are all words that can be used to describe this relatively small part of the city. Unique it certainly is, but in a very good way. While sitting enjoying afternoon tea, it is not too difficult to think about the days of old when this area would have been used by friars to engage with the community, or to the days when traders from ships visiting the harbour could sell their goods. The Merchant Quarter has always been about people, and today it has retained that personal touch. It is an absolutely must-visit place in the heart of Aberdeen.

Exploring

The Green

The history of this part of Aberdeen dates back to the pre-historic era when the first settlers arrived around 8,000 years ago. Tiny blades, made from local honey-coloured flint, were found by archaeologists during excavations of the area. Various groups of people would have worked the land, but it was probably not until the 13th century that a community was formed. Alison Cameron, archaeologist, says "This area of the city is now a busy hub of activity, with the railway station, the bus station and the shopping mall nearby. But of course in the 13th century it was quite different, probably more marginal in terms of the developing town of Aberdeen. The Carmelites would have chosen it for this reason; they tended to select places that were out of town a little."

The Green is located opposite Union Square Shopping Centre. The area can be accessed by crossing Guild Street from the main entrance of the shopping centre, or from Union Street, via Market Street.

The Merchant Quarter

A multi-million pound streetscape renewal project, opened in October 2010, marked a major reinvention of the Green. The streetscape of this area owes much of its charm to its vertically enclosed and narrow streets, which are partially surfaced in traditional granite flags, setts and kerbs. However, these had become fragmented over time. The improvement work that was undertaken to restore the streets and walkways for pedestrians and motorists has greatly improved the area. Trees and shrubs have been planted, with new outdoor seating and better lighting adding to the character of the area. With its many café-bars and boutique shops this area is a pleasant place to spend a few hours.

The official website of the Merchant Quarter provides details of shops, restaurants and hotels.
www.merchantquarter-aberdeen.com

The Whisky Walk

The Whisky Walk features the two-hundred-year-old Glen Garioch Distillery. After taking a visit to the distillery, which can be reached by bus from Aberdeen Bus Station, a variety of other Scottish whiskies can be sampled in the bars and pubs within the Merchant Quarter.

The Whisky Walk has 12 bars on the trail, all within two minutes' walk from each other. All of those bars are listed on the Merchant Quarter website.

Glen Garioch Distillery

The Garioch, pronounced 'geery', is a tract of richly fertile land, some 150 square miles in extent. Bounded by rolling hills, the quaint market town of Oldmeldrum, where the distillery stands, is 18 miles to the north-west of Aberdeen.

Cereal crops have been abundant in this area of Aberdeenshire for thousands of years, while the crystal springs that supply the Glen Garioch Distillery have also made the town famous for its beer. The distillery was founded in 1797 and is one of Scotland's oldest.

Details of opening times can be found on their website.
www.glengarioch.com

Oldmeldrum

Oldmeldrum, commonly known as 'meldrum', has a population of around 2,000 people. As well as the distillery, there are other attractions for the visitor. Each summer on the third Saturday in June, the town hosts the very popular 'Meldrum Sports'. The sports, which began in 1930, feature Highland Games, dancing, pipe bands, displays, stalls and a beer tent. To the north of the village is Meldrum House, a mansion and castle built in the 13th century. Haddo House, a stately home run by the National Trust for Scotland, is seven miles north-east of the village and is well worth a visit.

Daily buses run from Aberdeen Bus Station to Oldmeldrum.
www.aberdeenshire.gov.uk/publictransport

The National Trust for Scotland

The National Trust for Scotland looks after one world heritage site, 16 islands, almost 200,000 acres of countryside, seven national nature reserves, 26 castles, four battle sites and numerous other places of interest. All of these are listed on the National Trust for Scotland website.
www.nts.org.uk

PLAY A ROUND OF GOLF

Scotland's east coast is famous for many things, but probably none more than the game of golf, which took root in this area of Scotland as far back as the 15th century. Some of the finest, and most challenging, courses in the world are located around the north-east. The renowned 8th hole at Royal Aberdeen, a superb par 3, has no less than nine bunkers protecting the green. The only safe route is to drive straight down the middle, a daunting task on any links course.

The first documented mention of golf in Scotland appears in a 1457 Act of the Scottish Parliament. King James II prohibited the playing of the game of 'gowf', as it was known then, because it was a distraction from military training. Further reference to the game appears a few years later in 1471, when the game was described as "an unprofitable sport".

It was not until several centuries later that the modern game of golf became established. On 7 March 1744, the Honourable Company of Edinburgh Golfers was formed. The club drafted the first set of rules, the Articles and Laws in Playing at Golf, which are now preserved in the National Library of Scotland. Known as the Leith Rules, these formed the basis of the game as it is played today. One of the early rules stated "You are not to change the ball which you strike off the tee".

Ten years after the formation of the first golf club, 22 "Noblemen and Gentlemen" formed the Society of St Andrews Golfers. Adopting the rules set forth by their Edinburgh counterparts, the club at St Andrews later changed its name to the Royal and Ancient Golf Club of St Andrews, a name now recognised world-wide as the epitome of the sport today.

Although some minor changes have been made, most of the original rules of golf set out during the 18th century are still applicable today, with one exception. Originally, golf was played over 22 holes but, in 1764, the Links at St Andrews, later changed to the Old Course, was reduced to 18 holes. The reduction in holes gradually became accepted as the standard for golf courses around the world.

On the green at Royal Aberdeen

Golfing legends

A leading figure in the evolution of golf course design was legend Tom Morris (1821–1908). Born in St Andrews, the son of a weaver, he won the British Open four times, still holding the record as the oldest winner of the Championship at 46 years of age. Although his prowess on the course is unquestionable, it is his architecture of courses that has ensured his name lives on.

Morris assisted with the design of famous courses such as the Old and New Courses at St Andrews, Carnoustie, Nairn and Royal Dornoch. Although he was instrumental in the standardisation of the 18-hole course, perhaps more importantly he was responsible too for placing 'hazards' so that balls had to be played around them to reach the green!

Another giant who emerged in golf course design was James Baird. Born in Earlsferry, Fife, in 1870, Baird became a professional golfer in 1896 and pioneered the use of aluminium-headed putters. He was responsible for designing over 250 courses throughout the British Isles, including several links courses, many of which remain today.

Links courses

Links courses in Scotland offer the ultimate challenge to the golfer. Usually near the coast, these golf courses are often constructed around sand dunes with little trees or water features.

Gary Forbes, the PGA Professional at Murcar Links Golf Club in Aberdeen, comments "Aberdeen has a great choice for the visitor who wants to play a round or two of golf. Here at Murcar we have a fantastic links course.

"Our club was formed in 1908, with the first course opened in June 1909. The course is a great example of a typical north-east of Scotland links course. It was built around the local geography, utilising the natural environment. This makes it a challenge but also a joy to play. The course weaves around the sand dunes and grasses that dominate this area, fitting in with the natural contours of the land. Very little reshaping was done to the land, so playing the course is like playing through the natural landscape.

"Every single hole at Murcar is different and even the same hole has to be played differently, depending on the weather. Sometimes the wind comes from the north, but often there are strong cross winds coming off the sea. This means that the golfer will experience a different course every time he plays. Without doubt, playing Murcar is like playing a championship course.

A golf course on Deeside

"Everyone who plays here has a story to tell. Whether it be the ball taking a spectacular, but unusual, flight through the air or how many balls they lost in the wispy grass in the dunes, few people complete the course without a tale to take home with them.

"Murcar Links, with its par 71, frequently rates in the top 100 courses in the UK and is in the Visit Scotland top 40 Great Scottish Links Collection. Over the years, we have hosted many prestigious events, including pre-qualifying for the British Senior Open.

"The course is not for the faint hearted. To play it requires every shot in the book and, if the wind is up, a few more besides. From the tee on the third, it will become apparent what lies in store for the remainder of the round. On looking back from the green the golfer may be under the impression that he has just negotiated a lunar landscape!

"There are a few doglegs in wait. The first of these is hole six. The natural contours of the fairway will kick the ball left towards the green if it has been struck accurately from the tee. However, there is always a bunker lurking in wait for the inaccurate shot.

"No respite on this course, because at the seventh every piece of danger is visible.

It is for the thinking golfer to determine how to play the hole. Too far right and a lost ball or an impossible second shot will be the result. Too far left and a lost ball is again the likely outcome, or at the very least, a blind second shot over or around a gorse-covered dune.

"The other holes have their own difficulties. Finally, the danger is there to be seen from the tee of the last hole. An accurate drive will set up a simple second shot to a well-guarded green, but don't relax yet. There is also out of bounds around the car park and clubhouse.

"There is no doubt, this course is a challenge, but visitors love to play the course. People playing at Murcar enjoy the feeling of playing and exploring a true north-east links course."

Located next door to Murcar, southwards towards the city, lies an even greater challenge – the course at Royal Aberdeen. Hosts of the 2011 Walker Cup, the Royal Aberdeen Golf Club, founded in 1780, is the world's sixth-oldest golf club.

Royal Aberdeen is a classic links course – out through the sand dunes and back along a plateau. The first hole offers a wide fairway, slightly downhill from the elevated clubhouse. The second hole, a par 5, can be deceiving with its grassy hillocks that have high sand dunes on

In the bunker at Royal Aberdeen

PLAY A ROUND OF GOLF

the right. It can seem calm in the valley, but often the blustery winds coming from the North Sea necessitate low irons along the fairway.

The eighth is the course's signature hole. The club's website states "A par 3 that changes its spots to suit conditions, a 3 iron one day, a pitching wedge the next. Nine bunkers surround the green like a dragon's teeth and the only way home is straight down its throat."

Heading home at the tenth, with the wind most often coming from the south-west, Royal Aberdeen's back nine holes are quite different in appearance and nature from the seaward holes. Less undulating than the outward nine, the remaining holes have blind tee shots, hidden troughs and much more difficult putting surfaces to challenge the golfer.

In terms of disguised difficulty, there are few holes around the world that can beat the final hole at Royal Aberdeen. From the tee, the hole doesn't seem too difficult but this is a par 4 that aims to catch the over-confident or tired player. Most of the time the tee shot is into the wind with rough and gorse either side. The green is slightly raised and, like most other holes on this course, is well protected with bunkers. A classic hole to end a classic round of golf at one of the most prestigious golf clubs in the world.

On the beachfront

Continuing south from Royal Aberdeen, is the Kings Links Golf Club. Running parallel with the Aberdeen beachfront, and close to other leisure facilities such as cinemas, ice rinks and restaurants, this municipal course has a wide range of holes to test the most experienced golfer.

Similar to the other links courses in Aberdeen, the outward nine holes at Kings Links are played facing the north, with the inward nine holes played into the prevailing wind. However, such are the changeable weather conditions in this area of Scotland, that this is an often unpredictable course. Strong winds come off the North Sea and, because the course lies at sea-level, winds can whip around it, making tee shots unpredictable and, quite often, spectacular.

Of course, it is not only tee shots that test the aspiring golfer. Almost half of all shots on the golf course are actually played with a putter! It is little wonder then that the best way to reduce a handicap is to get some putting practice. At the Kings Links Golf Centre they believe that a golfer can only develop a consistently sound stroke when practising on a good putting surface. This is why they have installed an artificial putting surface, to complement their 56-bay floodlit driving range. With a PGA professional on hand, the Kings Links

Centre is open seven days a week for lessons or for the use of facilities.

Further down the coast from Kings Links, the most southerly of Aberdeen golf clubs is set in a legendary location on the south side of the city. Regardless of the challenge offered at the Balnagask Golf Club, this course will inspire and excite for many reasons other than the sport itself. For a start, there is the view over the city. Situated on a small headland, the view from many tees on the course, over Aberdeen harbour and the beach, is quite stunning. On a clear day it is possible to see some of the hills of the Grampian Mountains to the west.

In addition to the views, the course is built near to many important archaeological sites. Because of the position and view over the harbour, the Torry Battery was built in 1861, to defend Aberdeen during the war with France. Armed with 200 pound Armstrong guns, the battery could fire upon attacking ships nearing the city. Ruins of the battery still remain today and can be seen from many of the greens on the course.

Dominating the landscape in this part of the city is the Girdleness Lighthouse. Following the wrecking of a whaling ship in 1813 with the loss of 43 lives, the Shipmaster of Aberdeen ordered the building of a lighthouse to warn ships

off the rocks to the south of the city.

Both the Torry Battery and Girdleness Lighthouse form a picturesque backdrop to the Balnagask course. Playing to more than 6,000 yards, this gently undulating par 70 looks down over the city, and offers a challenging layout with demanding hollows, dips and unsuspecting strong overhead winds.

Other courses

If unpredictable weather conditions appeal to those who like the challenge of a typical links course, then Aberdeen can certainly meet those needs. However, sometimes it is good to take a break from the demands of a championship links course or from a course perched on top of the city.

Frank Coutts, Director of Golf at the Deeside Golf Club says "Aberdeen has tremendous links courses that attract hundreds of tourists every year. It is quite special to play on one of Aberdeen's links courses, especially Royal Aberdeen. However, Deeside can beat most of the other courses around here for its beauty. Also, Deeside doesn't get hammered by the weather like the coastal courses. Our course is much more sheltered, offering a softer challenge.

"Deeside Golf Course, situated four miles from the centre of Aberdeen, was founded

Royal Aberdeen

improve driving skills
at the Kings Links
Golf Centre

take a break from
links courses and play
the picturesque course
on Deeside

play a round on
the edge of the bay,
at Balnagask

enjoy
the challenging
championship course
at Royal Aberdeen

Highlights

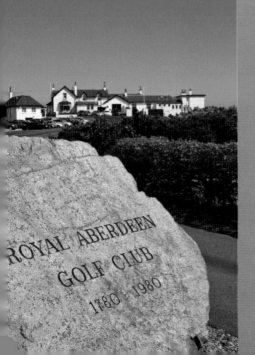

as a private club in 1903. Located on the banks of the River Dee, we have two courses: the 18-hole Haughton Course and the 9-hole Blairs.

"Amazing views, well-conditioned fairways and greens, and a stellar clubhouse all add up to a premier round of golf at our club, and we are more than willing to accept visitors. The Haughton course plays to 6,407 yards with a par of 70. The course includes two monstrous par 5s, while our par 4s and 3s will require accuracy and solid golf-course management to get a round with a good score."

Deeside, with its picturesque location, is one of three non-links courses in the Aberdeen area that offer a fantastic round of golf. The other two are Auchmill and Hazlehead.

Auchmill is the newest of courses in Aberdeen. Opened in 1975, originally as a nine-hole course, such was its popularity that the course was extended to 18 holes in 1989. The golf course is nestled between two major residential areas of the city and, because of its high location, the greens offer excellent views across the north part of Aberdeen.

Four miles west of the centre of Aberdeen lies Hazlehead Golf Club. With three picturesque courses set in mature woodland areas, and a pitch and putt course,

Hazlehead offers an excellent golfing experience. Described on the club website as having one of the best courses in the north-east of Scotland, the premier course provides a true test of skills, with gorse and woodland being the main hazards to any wayward shots.

The number two course at Hazlehead is ideal for higher handicap players because of its more open aspect. There is also an excellent nine-hole course, with wide fairways and much less rough, which is ideal for the beginner or visitor who hasn't played for a while. Many local champions started their golfing careers on the nine-hole at Hazlehead.

From the scenic beauty of the club on Royal Deeside, and the views offered from Balnagask, to the challenge and test of skill of the links courses on the coast, Aberdeen has a tremendous selection of courses. All within a short travelling distance from the city centre, and easily accessible by car or public transport, the golfing opportunities in this part of the north-east of Scotland are unrivalled. There can be very few places around the world that offer such diversity of golfing opportunities. It is little wonder then that Aberdeen's culture is steeped in golfing history, making this area an ideal choice for the explorer to sample a fine round or two of the gowf.

A diverse and beautiful range of courses await the golfer

Exploring

Murcar Links Golf Club

Murcar Links Golf Club is a members' club but it is keen to let visitors enjoy the course and facilities. The club is more than happy to accommodate individual golfers or groups. There is an online form, to be used for booking tee times.

Murcar Links Golf Club is approximately five miles north of Aberdeen on the A90 towards the Aberdeen Exhibition and Conference Centre (AECC). Pass the AECC and take a right at the next roundabout (where the A90 and B999 intersect). Head towards the North Sea, following the signs to the club, down a single-track road.
www.murcarlinks.com

Royal Aberdeen Golf Club

Royal Aberdeen is the sixth-oldest golf club in the world and offers a fantastic round of golf on the Balgownie course. Recently refurbished, Royal Aberdeen's clubhouse maintains the traditional ambience of a 'gentlemen's' club. With casual dining in the lounge, Royal Aberdeen's catering is there to be enjoyed after a great 18-holes.

Royal Aberdeen is located two miles north of Aberdeen and can be seen immediately after crossing the Bridge of Don on King Street. Turn right at the first set of traffic lights after crossing the Bridge of Don (Links Road) and then take the left fork approximately 50 yards further along the road.
www.royalaberdeengolf.com

Kings Links Golf Club

Kings Links 18-hole course is a traditional, well-established links course, running parallel with the Aberdeen beachfront and close to other leisure facilities and to Pittodrie Stadium, home of Aberdeen Football Club. The course has a wide range of holes, the longest being 502 yards with the shortest a 171 yard par 3.

The Kings Links Golf Club is located off Golf Road, opposite Pittodrie Stadium.
www.aberdeencity.gov.uk/sportaberdeen/facilities/golf

Balnagask Golf Club

The Balnagask Golf Course, located in the Torry area of Aberdeen, is a challenging coastal course with many small hills and undulations.

After crossing the Victoria Bridge on Market Street, follow Victoria Road until it joins St Fitticks Road, on the south of the city.
www.aberdeencity.gov.uk/sportaberdeen/facilities/golf

Auchmill Golf Club

Auchmill Golf Course is situated in the Northfield/Bucksburn area of the city. Set out originally as a nine-hole course run by Aberdeen City Council, the course was extended to 18 holes in 1989 and became a private members' golf club. However, visitors are very welcome at the club.

Auchmill Golf Course can be reached from Aberdeen's North Anderson Drive. Turn off at the Provost Rust roundabout, and follow Provost Rust Drive until the end of the road. Turn right into Bonnyview Drive.
www.auchmillgolfclub.co.uk

Deeside Golf Club

The panoramic views from the course, the welcoming atmosphere in the clubhouse and the well-stocked professionals' shop combine to provide an outstanding impression. Stepping onto the first tee confirms that an excellent decision has been made to play Deeside.

Deeside is located off the North Deeside Road (A93). From the city centre, take the A93 towards Braemar. At Bieldside, turn left onto Golf Road and follow the road to the clubhouse.
www.deesidegolfclub.com

Hazlehead Golf Club

Hazlehead offers three picturesque courses and a pitch-and-putt.

Designed by Alistair McKenzie, the golf architect better known for designing the Augusta National, the Number 1 course provides a true test of golf skills, with gorse and woodland being hazards. The second course, originally a nine-hole course, extended in the 1970s, has a more open aspect, making it suitable for those who want to brush up on their technique. The nine-hole course has wide fairways.

All courses are accessible from the main clubhouse, which is located off Hazlehead Avenue. From the town centre, head up Queens Road on the B9119. At the Kings Gate roundabout, take a left onto the narrow Hazlehead Avenue. Continue on this road until it ends at the clubhouse.
www.aberdeencity.gov.uk/sportaberdeen/facilities/golf

Kings Links Golf Centre

Whether it is to fill a few spare hours between rounds, or simply to brush up on driving or putting technique, a visit to the Kings Links Golf Centre is a must.

Their award-winning 3,000 square feet superstore, which is open seven days a week, offers an extensive range of leading golf equipment, clothes and accessories. Add to that the excellent tuition that is available for both locals and visitors, the floodlit driving range and the putting greens, and the centre is not to be missed.
www.craig-group.com/craig_group_leisure

Royal and Ancient

As golf's governing body, the R&A is responsible for writing the Rules of Golf, developed over more than 250 years. The R&A website has an excellent 'rule finder' to test the most ardent golf fan.
www.randa.org

173

PEOPLE AND PLACES

Over the centuries many famous and notorious people have visited Aberdeen, contributing to the evolution of the city as we see it today. From Robert the Bruce, whose armies marched into the city during the 14th century, to a wealth of authors, artists, engineers and royalty, Aberdeen really has been touched by the great and the good – and often by the bad too. The legacies left behind by those who have visited the city have resulted in a wealth of opportunities to excite the intrepid city explorer.

Aberdeen's motto is Bon Accord, which is French for 'good agreement'. Legend has it that the term came from an event that occurred in 1308, when Aberdonians aided the destruction of the 'castle' to prevent it from being re-used by the English when they were beaten back during the Scottish invasions of this period. Although not fully substantiated by historical evidence, the tradition that the motto was con-ceived in this way has stood the test of time, with Bon Accord now fully embedded into the very essence of the city.

It is likely that the first castle in Aberdeen was not actually located in the area now known as Castlegate, but on top of St Catherine's Hill in the Green. Historians and archaeologists believe that as the population of the young royal burgh started to grow, the castle was moved from the Green to the area now known as Castle Hill, which sits behind the Castlegate at the top end of Union Street. The first historical evidence that confirmed the castle was located on Castle Hill dates to 1264 when a sum of money was paid to Richard the Mason for carrying out repairs there. However, most of the historical evidence that confirms the existence of the structure comes during the period of the Wars of Independence.

King Edward I of England, known posthumously as Hammer of the Scots, attempted to take control over Scotland. During the latter part of the 13th century, many of Scotland's castles were under the control of the king, including Aberdeen's. The castle was handed back to the Scots in 1292 when Edward agreed that John Balliol should become King of Scotland.

However, conflict returned a few years later when, in March 1296, Edward's army returned to the city. An anonymous chronicler recorded that the soldiers had found *"bon chastell et bon ville sur la mer..."* (a good castle and a good town by the sea). Between 1306 and 1307, a garrison of Edward's army protected the castle in Aberdeen, led by the English soldier Gilbert Pecche.

In 1306, the famous Scot Robert the Bruce began his rebellion against the English, taking control of castles and towns occupied by Edward's men. By 1308 Bruce's troops reached Aberdeen and successfully took control of the stronghold. Documents from the 14th century refer to castle walls and ditches, but not to the actual structure itself, suggesting to historians that something happened to the building. Although the details are hotly debated, Aberdonians believe that the 'something' related to the help the locals provided to Robert the Bruce and his army by destroying the castle to prevent its re-use by the English.

Over the past 700 years many buildings have replaced the 14th-century castle on Castle Hill. Cromwell's troops built a bastion on the hill in the 1650s; army barracks were built in 1794, later demolished in 1969; and, in 1893, work started on the Salvation Army Citadel, which was completed in 1896 and still stands at the east end of the Castlegate.

Modelled on Balmoral Castle, Queen Victoria's Highland residence in Aberdeenshire, the Salvation Army Citadel is a spectacular building. It was completed when the granite industry in Aberdeen was at its peak. On a sunny day, mica crystals within the granite stone sparkle and, together with hundreds of other granite buildings in the city, have earned Aberdeen the nickname, the Granite City.

Granite stone

The history of granite in Aberdeen is a fascinating one. The north-east of Scotland's geological base is granite and for many years this hard stone has been used for building. As early as the 14th century buildings around Aberdeen were constructed, in part, with the stone. Drum Castle, built during the 1300s, and Crathes Castle, constructed in the 1500s, both have granite stone in their structures. However, it was not until much later that the demand for the material really took off.

The evolution of industry and commerce during the 18th century led to an unprecedented demand for granite. Greater horse traffic, with iron-shod cartwheels, increased the need for more durable materials for road building.

Rubislaw Quarry, late 19th century

Granite, because of its extremely hard properties, was ideal for this and Aberdeen began exporting the stone, particularly to London. Rubislaw Quarry, in what is now the west end of Aberdeen, became the epicentre of the granite industry in Great Britain.

Rubislaw Quarry, located at the Hill of Rubislaw about two miles west of the city centre, was opened in 1740. Aberdeen City Council decided that the stone from the quarry did not have suitable potential as a building material and so gave up the rights to work the land, selling those rights to local businessmen. Since then, an estimated six million tonnes of granite have been excavated from the quarry, resulting in a man-made hole that is now 450-feet deep.

One of the major turning points in the history of the quarry came with the introduction of steam as a power source. Granite stone is incredibly hard and difficult to 'work' so, in the 1830s, engineer Alexander MacDonald designed a steam-driven polishing machine that revolutionised large-scale production of the stone, making export commercially feasible.

By the end of the 19th century, Aberdeen had become the world leader in the granite trade. The city itself had hundreds of buildings constructed from the stone, from simple monuments to the elaborate New Town House. Architects John Smith and Archibald Simpson designed some of Aberdeen's best-known buildings, utilising the use of the stone in their creations. Waterloo Bridge in London, the terraces of the Houses of Parliament and the foundations of the Forth Rail Bridge have all been built with stone from Rubislaw Quarry.

The success of Aberdeen granite is all around to see. However, with the growing need for less-expensive building materials in the 20th century, such as concrete and steel, the demise of Rubislaw Quarry loomed. Although new technology helped to mechanise granite production, sadly it was not enough to save the industry. In 1971, after more than 200 years in operation, the quarry closed. Fortunately, the legacy of the industry lives on today, in the numerous buildings and structures around the city.

Marischal College is said to be the second-largest granite building in the world. Located on Broad Street, the building was formerly the seat of the ancient Marischal College and University of Aberdeen, which was founded in 1593. Designed by Archibald Simpson, construction of the modern college began in 1835. Additional work was completed in 1905 by Alexander Marshall Mackenzie when he extended the property with the local stone, with the result that the building is second only to the Escorial Palace in Spain.

Another fine example of the use of granite is evident within the Kirk of St Nicholas in the centre of Aberdeen. Originally constructed around 1157, the kirk was extended during the 15th and 19th centuries. After a fire in 1874, which destroyed the East Church together with the lead-clad timber tower, the church was rebuilt with a massive granite tower, which today stands prominently above the St Nicholas area of Aberdeen, providing a powerful reminder of the importance of the stone.

The invention of steam-powered polishing machines in the early part of the 19th century had a profound impact on one spin-off industry in Aberdeen. Although granite is very hard, it can be polished like marble. Taking the hard work out of polishing the stone, machines allowed craftsmen to produce memorial gravestones that are strong and impressive. All around the north-east of Scotland, in every cemetery, lie granite markers. Some are very small and simple, while others are elaborate and striking. Nellfield Cemetery is a great example of a city-centre cemetery that has a diverse

collection of polished granite stones. There is a fitting memorial to Alexander MacDonald on the wall of the cemetery, where a plaque has been positioned to pay tribute to the engineer who revolutionised the granite industry.

Important people

Of course, it is not only those associated with granite who have been recognised within the city. Commemorative plaques exist in many places around Aberdeen, paying tribute to those who have shaped the growth of the north-east town. For example, George Thompson, born in 1804, was the founder of the Aberdeen White Star Line, a famous shipping company.

Educated at Aberdeen Grammar School, George Thompson joined the Aberdeen office of the London Shipping Company but later set up his own business as a ship insurer. His business interests grew quickly and he soon became joint owner of vessels. His shipping routes extended to South America, Canada and China.

Thompson became Lord Provost of Aberdeen in 1847 and, on 8 September 1848, he welcomed two very special visitors to the city, people who would go on to contribute greatly to the shaping of Aberdeen and surrounding towns and villages: Queen Victoria and Prince Albert. The queen and the prince were travelling

The war memorial

to what would become the Highland home for generations of royalty, Balmoral Castle near Ballater.

There is an impressive monument to Albert, the Prince Consort, located on Union Terrace, in the garden area opposite His Majesty's Theatre. Unveiled by Queen Victoria in October 1863, the monument has Albert wearing the uniform of a Field Marshal and the insignia of the Order of the Thistle, the highest honour of Scotland. The badge motto is *"Nemo me impune lacessit"* (no one harms me with impunity).

The monument to Prince Albert is one of many fine examples of public art on display around the city. "Aberdeen has been a great conduit for creativity for centuries," says art historian and writer, Fiona Chapel. "For example, there is a wonderful piece of work called *Sea Fantasy*, which is located near to St Nicholas House on Broad Street. The sculptor, Thomas Bayliss Huxley-Jones, who was born in Aberdeen, created the piece. He went on to design many sculptures, including the figure of Helios, the sun god of Greek mythology, located in the courtyard of BBC Television Centre in London.

"The Castlegate Well, once a source of water for the city of Aberdeen, has a lead figure on top. Added in the late 18th century, the Mannie, depicting a half-clothed man, was erected by William Lindsay, a local goldsmith. The well-head was relocated to the Green in the 1850s but was returned to the Castlegate in 1972.

"Another very famous piece of artwork is the War Memorial on the corner of Schoolhill and Blackfriars Street, which depicts a lion, carved from silver-grey granite from the local Kemnay quarry. Designed by Aberdeen sculptor William Macmillan and the stonework by Arthur Taylor, the sculpture was unveiled by King George V in September 1925 when he opened the Cowdray Hall and Art Museum. Taylor also carried out the granite carving of the Greek goddess Hygeia, which stands in Duthie Park.

"A poignant reminder of life and death, not from war but from industrial disaster, can be found within the grounds of Hazlehead Park in Aberdeen. The memorial, by Scottish artist Sue Jane Taylor, is to the men killed in the Piper Alpha disaster on 6 July 1988. Piper Alpha was a North Sea oil production platform that began production in 1976. An explosion and resulting fire destroyed it, killing 167 men, with only 61 survivors. Sue Jane Taylor had spent time the previous year researching the lives and work of oilmen in the north-east of Scotland. The memorial can be found near to the Queen Mother Rose Garden in the park.

"Composers and authors have also contributed to Aberdeen's heritage. Ronald Center, born in 1913, who lived in the Elmbank area of the city, is remembered as a composer of string quartets and piano works, particularly for the choral piece *Dona Nobis Pacem*.

"Lord Byron was a British poet and a leading figure in the Romantic Movement. Born in 1788 and educated at Aberdeen Grammar School, George Gordon Byron, at the age of ten, inherited the Barony of Byron of Rochdale. Amongst his many masterpieces is *Don Juan*, a poem that ranks as one of the most important long poems ever published in Britain. Regarded by early Victorians as 'somewhat shocking', Byron has reflected on his contemporary world in this epic piece of writing.

"Another contemporary piece of work can be found on the upper storey of the St Nicholas Centre. *Two*, an abstract relief in bronze panels, is by Scottish artist Gavin Scobie. Regarded as one of Scotland's most important contemporary sculptors, Scobie, born in Edinburgh in 1940, was inspired by the Nigerian Nok

culture, considered to be the earliest of life-size terracotta figures.

"Scobie also created an interesting piece of work that is located in the Tyrebagger forest on the outskirts of Aberdeen. The piece, called *Tyrebagger Circle*, is set back off one of the forest paths in an area of woodland. The work consists of three concentric wooden fences each progressively higher towards the centre. The idea developed from earlier gallery pieces as well as from his interests in Greek theatres. Tyrebagger wood is a mature forest where several sculptures have been distributed throughout the area. Connected by a series of paths, it is a wonderful place to go to see great pieces of contemporary work."

Whether it be to enjoy the variety of sculptures that are abundant through Aberdeen's city centre, or to watch granite buildings come to life as they sparkle on a sunny day, taking a little time out to explore the plaques and historical venues of Aberdeen is a great way to appreciate the work of those who have shaped the city and its culture. Aberdeen has many people to celebrate, from those who have formed businesses that influenced city life to those who were born in Aberdeen and went on to achieve great things in their field.

Charles George Gordon, at the Robert Gordon University

explore the granite
buildings around
the city

search for commemorative
plaques of politicians,
engineers, builders and
artists who contributed
to the culture
of Aberdeen

follow the sculpture trail to see fine examples of traditional and contemporary works of art

trek the sculpture trails in Tyrebagger forest, just outside the city

Highlights

Exploring

Aberdeen's people and places

Commemorative plaques are distributed around Aberdeen, to remember those who have had a significant influence in the shaping of the city.

Aberdeen City Council has produced an excellent leaflet, *A guide to Aberdeen's commemorative plaques*, which references over 80 plaques and includes a city map with the locations of many of them. The leaflet states "From the nineteenth century plaques have been erected in Aberdeen often through the auspices of individuals or societies. These plaques are described as 'non-standard'. In the 1970s, the City Council introduced a degree of regularity, standardising most plaques erected to commemorate people as a distinctive round plaque design, whilst court plaques commemorating streets of historical importance are rectangular with a domed top edge."

Leaflets can be downloaded from the council's website.
www.aberdeencity.gov.uk

Aberdeen's sculpture trail

There is a diverse collection of sculptures and memorials around Aberdeen. Ranging from traditional granite pieces to more contemporary works by modern artists, these commemorate various leading figures and events that have touched the city. Whether in remembrance or simply to mark an occasion, these fine examples of artwork are there to be enjoyed.

Aberdeen City Council has published a leaflet to help those who wish to explore the numerous pieces of public art around the city. The leaflet contains reference to 19 pieces and there is a map with their locations.
www.aberdeencity.gov.uk/trails

Tyrebagger sculpture trail
Sculptures were first installed in the
Tyrebagger woods in 1994, as part of a
pilot project led by Forestry Commission
Scotland. Artists were invited to create work
that would reflect the north-east of Scotland.
The intention was to encourage local people,
and visitors, to take a fresh look at their
surroundings and to consider the relationship
between nature and culture.

Tyrebagger lies a little more than five miles
north-west of Aberdeen. Take the A96 road
from the city centre, towards the airport.
Continue on the A96 past the airport
junction, heading towards Inverness.
About a mile on, turn left onto the B979,
which is signposted to Kirkton of Skene.
www.forestry.gov.uk

Hazlehead Park
The memorial to the 167 men killed in the
Piper Alpha disaster can be found within
Hazlehead Park. Originally part of the
Freedom Lands granted to the city in 1319,
this 450-acre park lies on the outskirts of
Aberdeen, in the west end. The park has
many attractions including pitch and putt, a
golf course, football pitches, large grass areas
and woods for walking and cycling. The park
has a wonderful rose garden and numerous
other plants and trees. There is a children's
play area and a small zoo within the park.

Home to the annual Highland Games, the
park can be reached from either King's Gate
or Queen's Road. The access road to the park
is at the roundabout where these roads meet.
www.aberdeencity.gov.uk

Ask any local the question "where is the best place to find a great walk?" and they are likely to reply "Bennachie".

Bennachie is not a hill itself, but rather a prominent range of hills in Aberdeenshire, located about 25 miles from the centre of Aberdeen. It is one of the most popular and best-loved attractions for locals and visitors. Whether it is for spotting rare wildlife, exploring the history of the area, or simply enjoying a short trek, a walk to the top of the many peaks in the range can be invigorating and rewarding.

The north-east of Scotland, particularly around the city of Aberdeen, is pre-dominantly flat, with fertile farming land. However, protruding from the area around Inverurie, to the north-west of the city, and dominating the landscape for miles around, are the peaks of the range collectively referred to as Bennachie.

The highest peak in the Bennachie range is Oxen Craig, at a little over 1,700 feet. However, the most prominent summit, and the one closest to the city, is Mither Tap. At 1,690 feet, spectacular views across the north-east of Scotland can be seen from its distinctive granite top.

Many believe that the peak of Mither Tap had significant importance to the people of the Iron Age. This theory is supported by the numerous stone circles around this part of the north-east of Scotland. It is perhaps the shape of the summit that caught the attention, for the profile of the hill and its top resembles the shape of a female breast, hence the name Mither Tap (mother's breast in Scots).

Climbing the Mither Tap is reasonably easy until the final section which passes through an entrance corridor in a massive, but ruinous, outer and inner wall – the remains of an Iron Age Fort (circa 500BC). Loose rocks from the ruins of the fort make this route a little tricky, especially when the wind is strong. Care is needed when ascending over these rocks at the top, but the reward when the summit is reached is certainly worth the effort.

Although most people choose to explore the Mither Tap, there is much on offer from the other peaks in the range. From Oxen Craig, the highest peak, it is possible to see some of the mountains in the Cairngorms range, including Lochnagar.

Interesting places to explore

There are many redundant granite quarries on the hills of Bennachie. The largest quarry, which is south of the Garbit Tap (1,530 feet), was known as the English Quarry, because it was an

English company that operated it during the 1800s. It sent the quarried granite to London, to build part of the Thames Embankment.

There is another fine example of a quarry on the slopes of Little Oxen Craig, which was opened by Andrew Fordyce in the mid-1800s. He operated a lintel quarry and, although the company ceased trading after a severe flood washed away access roads, there are still some examples of granite lintels to be found on the hill.

Further east of Little Oxen Craig is Craigshannoch (1,570 feet). There is an exquisite ridge on the top of this hill. There are two tors east of the ridge, and the space between them is known as Little John's Length. It was believed that a friendly giant, named Jock o' Bennachie, lived on the mountain range. His bed was said to be between the two tors, a distance of about 600 feet!

Folklore abounds in this part of the north-east of Scotland. The path from the Rowantree Car Park to Mither Tap follows part of the trail known as the Maiden Causeway. Possibly used by ancient people to cart materials up the hill when building the fort at the top, the causeway is the subject of a much-loved legend. The lovely Maiden of Drumdurno, on the eve of her wedding, was baking oatcakes, singing merrily as she worked. She looked up and saw a handsome stranger, who wagered

her that he could build a causeway right up to the top of the hill from her cottage at the bottom, in the time that it would take her to finish baking. Thinking that this was idle talk, she promised her hand and heart in marriage as a reward if he could indeed achieve his remarkable claim. At twilight, as her meal was almost baked, she looked up and saw a causeway right to the top of the hill. Realising that the stranger was Satan himself, the maiden fled into the woods. Although he caught the frightened lass, her screams for help caused him to turn her to stone. Today, the Maiden Stone stands at the roadside between the Rowantree Car Park and Chapel of Garioch.

Dating from around AD700–800, the Maiden Stone is an excellent example of Pictish sculptured stone. The mirror and comb carved into it are believed by some to resemble the maiden's girdle and baking board, while the crack near to the top of the stone is thought to be the mark of Satan's hand.

The Picts were probably the first group of people to settle around the hills of Bennachie. But another group has also left its mark on the landscape in this area. In the early 19th century, rural society was changing. Landowners were developing their estates and needed income from their land to help finance their plans. Agriculture and farming of the land meant that many rural

communities were evicted, resulting in them trying to find places to settle.

The Colonists

The Bennachie Colonists were a group of people who chose to make their homes on the foothills around the range. Arriving about 1825, the colonists came from as far afield as Inverness in the north and Fife in the south. They consisted of skilled stone workers, quarriers and thatchers, and made their living from the land, often killing deer from the 'Bennachie larder'.

Local lairds divided up the land occupied by the Bennachie Colonists. Despite the efforts of a growing population of colonists, their expulsion was legalised in 1859 when the Commonty of Bennachie was legally split up amongst local landowners.

A fascinating reminder of the colonists on Bennachie has been preserved for all to enjoy. The remains of many of the houses still exist today, as well as fruit bushes, laurel and honeysuckle that the colonists had planted. The Colony Trail, a walking route around the preserved sites, starts at the Bennachie Visitor Centre and is one of the most popular walks in the area.

The Bennachie Visitor Centre

The Bennachie Visitor Centre, which is run by Aberdeenshire Council Ranger Service and is managed by the Bennachie Centre Trust, is a dedicated visitor facility that

has permanent and changing exhibitions that interpret the heritage of the hills. Alison Sutherland, Countryside Ranger for the Garioch area, comments "The centre was opened in 1995, by the Prince of Wales, to provide information and assistance to the public. People can come into the centre and delve into the history of the hill, how it was formed, learn a little about the biodiversity that exists and even play with some of the interactive displays we have on offer.

"Our role as rangers is to help the public and school groups to learn about the hills around here and what they have to offer. There are many features to the hills that people don't always appreciate so we do guided walks and talks about the geology and geography and about the wonderful wildlife that is present.

"The amount of migrating birds that can be seen here in spring is fantastic. Loads of different warblers, woodpeckers and ospreys too. We have a bird hide in the centre, so people can often see the great spotted woodpecker and red squirrels from the hide.

"We get lots of different people coming to visit the hills around this area. From dog walkers to bird-spotters, and from horse riders to mountain bikers, the hills are great for many different pastimes. One day, a colleague met a woman doing her yoga and on another occasion she came

Entrance to the fort at the top of the hill

across an elderly gentleman at the top, who was relaxing in the sun doing his crossword."

To help people access the features on the hill, there are many trails across the 25 square miles that make up the Bennachie range. The Discovery Trail, designed for all abilities, meanders through the forest and abounds with the sights, smells and sounds of the woodland. The trail has various posts along the route that are suitable for young children, for taking animal rubbings. The Quarry Trail, which starts at the Back o' Bennachie Car Park, leads to the top of Little Oxen Craig, continuing over Oxen Craig to Mither Tap. The trail passes some of the old quarry sites. One of the most spectacular routes, and probably the most popular with visitors, is the Timeline Trail. Starting at the visitor centre, this route leads directly to Mither Tap, over landscape that was formed more than 10,000 years ago.

Many of the paths and trails over Bennachie are maintained by Forestry Commission Scotland (FCS), who work with a voluntary group known as the Bailies of Bennachie. Working closely with the FCS, the Bailies undertake research on the social and natural history of the hill and restoration and conservation projects. Jackie Cumberbirch, a Conservation Ranger with the FCS, and herself a Bailie, says "The Bailies were formed in 1973 to

help protect the hill and to learn more about the history and wildlife of the landscape and to work with landowners to help protect this unique area.

"The Bailies were started by two or three people, really to clean up the rubbish that had accumulated on the paths. Today, with over 32,000 members, we are involved in lots of diverse projects, from practical work, research, music events and education. We are keen to involve anyone interested in Bennachie.

"The visitor centre at Bennachie was funded by several organisations, including the Bailies of Bennachie. The building has been designed so that it fits into the Scots pine woodland that surrounds it, and it mimics the Iron Age fort found on top of Mither Tap. The centre was opened by our most famous Honorary Bailie, HRH Prince Charles."

Whether it is simply to enjoy a stroll up Mither Tap, or indeed explore more fully the other great peaks in the range, or to look out for the abundance of wildlife, Bennachie has something for everyone. This is truly an area of variety. With folklore about giants and the devil, geographical features unique to the north-east and purple heather in abundance, a trip to Bennachie is a must-do for the explorer in this part of Scotland.

watch red squirrels from
the visitor centre

climb to the top
of Mither Tap

visit the nearby stone circle at Easter Aquhorthies and reflect on the reasons for such an elaborate construction

follow the trail from the Donview car park, up and over Millstone Hill, for spectacular views of the Don Valley

Highlights

The Lord's Throat

Red squirrel

Easter Aquhorthies stone circle

Great spotted woodpecker

Exploring

The Bennachie Visitor Centre

Take the A96 from Aberdeen to Inverurie. About three miles past Inverurie, the road to Chapel of Garioch is signposted on the left. At Chapel of Garioch, the road branches left and right; take the left fork. Continue on this road until the Bennachie Visitor Centre is signposted on the right.

Many of the trails start from the car park at the visitor centre. The Mither Tap Timeline Trail, which is three miles long, is quite arduous, especially near to the top. Allow about three hours for the return journey.

For more information and opening times of the visitor centre, visit the Aberdeenshire Council website.
www.aberdeenshire.gov.uk

Bennachie Donview Car Park

The Donview Car Park is set in a very picturesque area, with picnic tables, toilets, and information about the hill. This is the best place to begin the long-distance Mither Tap Heather Brig Trail. This six-mile trail passes over Millstone Hill to ascend the southern face of Mither Tap. After crossing the valley at Heather Brig, there are splendid views of Donside, stretching over the Lord's Throat, a local unmarked road.

There is a shorter and much easier trail from this car park. The Millstone Trail winds through the forest before climbing onto

Millstone Hill. From the top, panoramic views of the whole Bennachie range can been seen.

This car park is located off the Lord's Throat. From the road that leads to the Bennachie Visitor Centre, continue south, until the Lord's Throat is signposted on the right.

Bennachie Rowantree Car Park

This car park is accessible from Chapel of Garioch. Instead of taking the left fork to the visitor centre, take the right fork in the village. Continue past the Maiden Stone (on the left) to the car park.

The Mither Tap Maiden Causeway Trail starts from this car park. The return journey is about four miles long and should take the average person about three hours to reach the top.

Back o' Bennachie Car Park

Continuing along the road from the Rowantree Car Park is the Back o' Bennachie Car Park. From here, it is possible to access the Working Wood Trail, a two-mile route that passes through a working forest.

This car park is also the place to begin the exciting Mither Tap Quarry Trail. There are several barbeque sites close to the car park, ideal for a picnic. The longest route to the top of Mither Tap, this trail passes over Little Oxen Craig, Oxen Craig and Craigshannoch. The views along the six-mile route are spectacular.

Forestry Commission Waymarkers

Location grid references can be found on the back of each waymarker on the hill.

The Bailies of Bennachie

The Bailies of Bennachie were formed over 40 years ago as a voluntary conservation society. With the objective of encouraging and stimulating the public's interest in the range, the Bailies are an active group that maintains footpaths and rights of way, and undertakes promotional activities.

For more information about the work of the Bailies, visit their website.
www.bailiesofbennachie.co.uk

Pictish stone and stone circles

There are many Pictish stones in the area around Bennachie. These were carved from AD400 to AD900 and demonstrate the art of the Picts. The symbols on the stones are drawn from a 'catalogue of symbols' used by the Picts, and are repeated at different sites across Scotland.

Stone circles around this area date from before 2000BC and were probably built by the first farmers as places to meet to conduct rituals according to phases of the moon. An excellent example of a stone circle near to Bennachie is the Easter Aquhorthies Stone Circle.

The Maiden Stone

Located on the road to the Rowantree Car Park, the Maiden Stone is a fine example of Pictish art. Every face of the tough granite slab has been cut back to form a series of complex designs and symbols, conveying important messages to the local inhabitants.

SPORT AND LEISURE

As a city that is nestled between two major Scottish rivers, with a beachfront that runs for two miles and Britain's highest mountains only two hours away, it is little surprise that Aberdeen has many sporting and leisure opportunities. With a professional football team in the Scottish Premier League, two universities with very active sports clubs and a wealth of activities from fishing to windsurfing, Aberdeen offers the visitor a wide range of sporting challenges and leisure pursuits.

Aberdeen beach is two miles long. From Footdee at the southern end to the local nature reserve at the Bridge of Don, the sands and beachfront attract visitors, tourists and locals. Many local people walk their dogs or simply enjoy a nice leisurely stroll along the waterfront. Visitors to the city marvel at the beautiful sands and, even on a day when the weather is not good, the beachfront is never empty. For others, a much more energetic time at the beach can be found.

Aberdeen Kayak Club, founded in 1976, is one of the focal points for the development of canoe sport in the north-east of Scotland. Although the club is primarily involved with recreational river paddling, skills can be developed in the surf off Aberdeen beach, particularly during the summer months. Often, on a Saturday or

Sunday morning, paddlers can be found out past the breakwaters alongside more ambitious kayakers.

Windsurfing is another popular sport at the beach. Professional instructors are in attendance most weekends to teach complete beginners as well as those wanting to learn more about 'carve gybes', loops and other freestyle tricks.

Football in Aberdeen

Whether the beachfront is about taking a stroll or for the excitement of surfing the breaking waves, an unmistakable landmark that can be seen by everyone at the beach is Pittodrie, home to Aberdeen Football Club (AFC). Formed in 1903 from the merger of three city clubs (Aberdeen, Victoria United and Orion), the club played its first match in August 1903 against Stenhousemuir.

In 1904 Aberdeen Football Club was elected to the new and expanded First Division. Although times of war halted competitive football in Scotland, the post-war years saw the club progressing steadily, winning several domestic trophies. However, it was not until the 1970s and 1980s that AFC made their mark on national and international football.

Pittodrie stadium

Willie Miller, voted the greatest Aberdeen player of all time in a 2003 poll to mark the club's centenary, reflects "I came to Aberdeen in 1971, as a professional football player, and ended up playing for 20 years.

"We had a few good years during the 1970s, but the best years at Aberdeen were those of Alex Ferguson's time. Sir Alex came to the club in 1978 and remained for eight years. During the 1980s we won 13 major trophies, which was extraordinary.

"Our biggest achievement came in 1983 when we won the European Cup Winners' Cup. We went into the final quite confident in our ability. A few of us were establishing ourselves in the Scottish international team, so we had a lot of experience playing big matches. We beat Real Madrid 2–1 after extra time, to lift the much-coveted trophy. It is amazing now, to think that Aberdeen Football Club is written on that trophy, alongside clubs such as Barcelona and Real Madrid.

"The one thing that I hadn't realised about winning a major competition was how it would change the club's profile and how it would change our lives. We all became internationally known, rather than just domestic champions. Of course, Sir Alex Ferguson went on to achieve tremendous success with Manchester United."

Another legend in Scottish football, who also ended up at Manchester United, was Denis Law. The son of an Aberdeen trawlerman, Law was born in the 1950s and played for the Aberdeen Lads' Club. He later signed for Huddersfield Town, at the age of 15, and became the youngest player ever to represent the club as an amateur footballer.

Denis Law's football career progressed at a great pace. He moved to Manchester City in 1960, in a record-breaking £55,000 deal. Before long, the Italian club, Torino, spotted the talented Scot and, after signing for them, Law found himself playing against the best in Europe. However, a season later, Manchester United paid £115,000 for the striker to join their ranks and Law teamed up with legendary manager Matt Busby.

Although Denis Law never played football at Pittodrie, the match of his life did take place in Aberdeen. Only a few months after signing for Manchester United, Law married Diana Thomson at Holburn West Church in the city centre in December 1962.

A sporting city

It is not only football that has produced great sporting heroes in Aberdeen. The Granite City has had many fine golfers through the decades. The Society of Golfers in Aberdeen was established in 1780 and since that time it has nurtured

many local and national champions. In 1999, the very best of those players joined the world-class elite in golfing.

Paul Lawrie won the Open Championship at Carnoustie in 1999, marking an unforgettable moment in Aberdeenshire's sporting success. Lawrie joined Banchory Golf Club in 1986 as a 17-year-old assistant to the club professional, Doug Smart. Serving under the watchful eyes of the professional at the club, Lawrie quickly gained in confidence and competence. He won the Scottish Assistants' Championship and the Scottish Under-25 Championship in 1990, going from strength to strength in the following years, until his greatest achievement in front of a Scottish crowd at Carnoustie.

Golf and football are two sports that have brought glory to Aberdeen for decades. But many other sporting greats from the city have gone on to reach the pinnacle of international success in their chosen field. The Aberdeen Sports Village was opened in 2009 and houses the city's sporting hall of fame. The Aberdeen Sports Council agreed that there should be 21 inaugural members of the hall of fame, marking 21 years of the council.

The 21 Aberdonian members selected were: Harry Bannerman (golf), Bill Berry (judo), Anne Robb Boyle (skiing), Martin Buchan (football), David Carry

(swimming), Neil Cochran (swimming), Chris Cusiter (rugby), Tony Dawson (badminton), Elaine Farquharson-Black (golf), Stephanie Forrester (athletics), Dennis Hay (hockey), Donny Innes (rugby), Denis Law (football), Paul Lawrie (golf), Graham Leggat (football), Linda Lesperance (curling), Ian McCrae (rugby), Sandy Pirie (golf), Frank Robertson (cricket), Colin Smith (cricket) and DWC Smith (rugby).

The Aberdeen Sports Village is the premier sports facility in the north-east of Scotland. The complex incorporates a wide range of amenities including a large sports hall (the size of nine badminton courts), a full-sized indoor football pitch, and an indoor athletics facility with fully equipped areas for long- and triple-jumping, high jump and pole vault. A fitness suite is also available, with a wide range of modern gym equipment.

It is not only sports venues within the city that generate challenges for sporting types. Within easy reach of the city are the hills and mountains of the Cairngorm range, suitable for the pursuit of everything from skiing to fishing. Aberdeen skier Anne Robb was called by the British Olympic Association and invited to represent Britain at the Winter Olympics in 1976.

take out a permit
and spend a day fishing
on the River Don

try snow sports in
the nearby mountains,
or even in the city

play a round of golf
at one of the many courses
in the city

watch the Dons
play a football match
at Pittodrie

Highlights

Coming from a family of skiing enthusiasts, Anne first took to the slopes of Glenshee as an eight-year-old. She represented both Aberdeen and the Scottish Ski Club before joining the Scottish team, sweeping to victory in the Scottish Championships in 1974.

Although the best places around the north-east for skiing are definitely to be found in the mountains, there are also opportunities to practise in more urban locations. The Aberdeen Snowsports Centre, which opened under new management in 2007, is based at Garthdee, near to the Bridge of Dee in the south of the city. The centre, which has a plastic ski slope, a dedicated tubing slope, lighting and ski lifts, offers tuition in skiing, snowboarding and tubing (whizzing down a slope in a large inflatable ring).

Near to the Snowsports Centre at Garthdee is one of two universities in Aberdeen. The Robert Gordon University, which is moving most of its facilities to the new campus at Garthdee, has recently invested over £11 million in a state-of-the-art sports facility which is open to the public. With its 25-metre pool, climbing wall, fully equipped gym and large sports hall, the sports complex is a great resource for staff, students and the wider community.

The Dee and the Don

Aberdeen University Sports Association is very active in the city. In fact, the university has 58 clubs, with university medals coming to Aberdeen in sports such as boxing, shooting, climbing, golf, fencing, volleyball and rowing.

The Aberdeen University Boat Club is the largest and one of the most successful university clubs in the city. Founded in 1870, the club is located on the banks of the River Dee, near to Menzies Road. The club is open to members of the public as well as students studying in the north-east.

Anglers from all over the world visit the north-east of Scotland to fish for salmon on the rivers Dee and Don. The River Dee is one of the big classic salmon rivers in Scotland, noted by enthusiasts as a great place for fly fishing, with many fishing experts considering it to be the best spring salmon river in the world.

Salmon stock numbers increase in the lower parts of the river, near to Aberdeen, until the water warms in spring, when large volumes of fish head upstream, often reaching Ballater and Braemar some 60 miles west from the lower reaches. The fishing season on the river runs from February through to mid-October for salmon, and from April to September for brown trout and sea trout.

Rowing on the River Dee

The River Don is also excellent for fishing, particularly for brown trout. Referred to as "the finest wild brown trout stream in Europe", the river enjoys the benefit of a Scottish Executive Brown Trout Protection Order, making it ideal for conservation fishing.

Scottish River Champion, and himself a resident of Aberdeen, Mike Cordiner comments "There is easily accessible brown-trout fishing all the way up from slightly above the tidal stretch on the River Don, near the Brig o' Balgownie, up to Dyce, which is on the outskirts of Aberdeen.

"All fishing in the area is permit controlled. A visiting angler is able to get a permit from the Aberdeen District Angling Association for about £70 for seven days.

"Fishing on the River Don is probably the best in Europe, particularly for brown trout, probably because of the landscape that the river flows through. Up at the top, where the river has its source, there is a lot of clean fresh water that flows through rocky fast-flowing areas. The water then slows considerably near to Inverurie, about 16 miles from the city, where rich nutrients in the soil leach into the river, which helps to promote weed growth in the river. Well-fed trout can grow up to 10 pounds, with three to four pounds being the normal.

"The evening is a great time for fishing on the River Don. The larger trout will come out to feed just before it gets dark.

"A few miles across the city is the River Dee, which is great for salmon and sea trout. The Dee is much faster-flowing than the Don, and there are fewer slow, deep pools and it is less affected by sediment. Although the best salmon are usually found in the middle reaches of the Dee, near to Banchory, it is possible to get fish on the outskirts of the city, probably around Peterculter.

"As well as the great river fishing, Aberdeenshire has lots of excellent stocked fisheries, which offer a great day out for the whole family. Rainbow trout and brown trout are usually found in fisheries that are only 30 to 40 minutes' drive from town. Many of the fisheries have equipment for hire, so you don't actually need to bring your own gear."

The abundance of sporting and leisure opportunities around the north-east of Scotland and within Aberdeen make this area truly unique. A visit to the city is not complete until at least a walk along the beachfront has been experienced. For the more discerning sporting type, there are numerous opportunities for surfing, skiing, fishing or hillwalking.

Trout fishing on the river

Wall climbing at the university sports centre

Surfing at Aberdeen beach

Exploring

Kayaking

Aberdeen Kayak Club has an active programme of events and it offers training sessions, either in a local pool, on the river, or at sea. For more details, visit their website.
www.aberdeenkayakclub.org.uk

Windsurfing

North Surf is one of the newest water-sports shops in the north-east of Scotland, offering equipment hire, advice on the best locations and professional tuition. More details can be found on their website.
www.northsurf.co.uk/school

Aberdeen Football Club

Formed in 1903, Aberdeen Football Club is the only club in Aberdeenshire that is in the Scottish Premier League. With its home ground at Pittodrie, just off the Beach Promenade, the first team play every other weekend from August to May. The official website of the club has links to their online shop and it is possible to buy tickets for their matches online. For more information about fixtures, the club's history and about Pittodrie Stadium, visit their website.
www.afc.co.uk

Pittodrie is located on Golf Road, which is about 15 minutes' walk from the city centre. There is a large car park and also plenty of parking available on the Beach Promenade.

Aberdeen Sports Village

Open to the public every day, the sports village is located on Linksfield Road, which is off King Street. It offers a wide range of activities, from the fitness gym to an indoor football pitch. For membership details or for pay-as-you-go prices and opening times, visit the website.
www.aberdeensportsvillage.com

Skiing in Scotland

If skiing is the thing that appeals most, then no trip to the north-east of Scotland is complete without a visit to one of the ski centres. Although there are several centres in Scotland, the nearest to Aberdeen are the Lecht and Glenshee.

At a little over 2,000 feet above sea level, amid the beauty of the eastern Cairngorms, the Lecht Activity Centre is situated in the heart of Scotland's largest national park. Twelve lifts, including a chairlift, take skiers and snowboarders up the hills to enjoy breathtaking descents to the day lodge far below. The Lecht is ideal for the novice skier but it is also the place to go when the other centres in the area are closed – often the Lecht will have accessible runs when the weather is too bad at other places. The Lecht is open all year, with a wide range of summer-fun activities on offer.

Glenshee boasts the most extensive skiing and snowboarding facilities in Scotland, with 22 lifts and 36 runs that offer an amazing diversity of natural terrain for all standards of skier and snowboarder.

The Aberdeen Snowsports Centre is the place to go for all-year skiing and snow-boarding. Located off Garthdee Road, the centre offers a range of different activities and events for all abilities.
www.lecht.co.uk
www.ski-glenshee.co.uk
www.skiaberdeen.com

Robert Gordon University

This world-class sports centre, which is open to the public, is ideal for those who want to tone up in the gym or take part in an indoor wall-climbing challenge or racket sport. Located on Garthdee Road, a short drive from the city centre, there is ample parking nearby. For more information, visit their website.
www.rgu.ac.uk

Rowing on the River Dee

Aberdeen Boat Club is Scotland's largest rowing club and one of the longest established clubs in the UK. Members of the club enjoy some of the best rowing facilities and boat fleets in the country. Founded in 1865, and catering for all abilities, the club has a thriving membership of more than 200 people. More information about opening times, tuition and membership can be found on their website.
www.abc-dee.co.uk

Fishing

Fishing offers relaxation, excitement and challenge. The north-east of Scotland, with its two famous rivers and numerous fish farms, is a haven for well-practised and amateur anglers alike.

The Aberdeen and District Angling Association has an excellent website where local information about river-fishing can be found. Tips and hints about the best places to visit, together with news about permits, can all be found on their website.
www.adaa.org.uk

PARKS, PETALS AND PIPES

Aberdeen is renowned for its beauty and open spaces, with some of the best green areas of any Scottish city. Within the 45 parks in the city there are over two million roses, 11 million daffodils and three million crocuses! Such is the beauty of this north-east townscape that Aberdeen has won Britain in Bloom's Best City category ten times. For people who are seeking peace and tranquillity or those looking for sporting adventure, Aberdeen's parks and open spaces are never far away.

Britain in Bloom is an important competition for villages, towns and cities across Great Britain. First established in 1963, and now run by the Royal Horticultural Society (RHS), "Bloom" as it is known, encourages locals to clean up their villages and towns and to plant flowers, shrubs and trees to enhance the beauty of their environment. Judges award achievements in three key areas: horticultural achievement, environmental responsibility, and community participation.

The idea of Britain's annual competition was conceived by Roy Hay MBE, a horticultural journalist. When holidaying in France he was impressed by President de Gaulle's orders to brighten up the country,

resulting in the French Tourist Authority setting up *Fleurissement de France*, an annual competition now called *Concours des villes et villages fleuris*. Hay approached the British Tourist Authority and, together with other interested parties, set up Britain in Bloom.

Aberdeen has had an impressive record since the conception of Britain in Bloom in 1963. The city has won Best City ten times, the overall Scotland in Bloom competition 20 times, and the International Cities in Bloom award.

Although the annual competition organised by the RHS is an important accolade for Aberdeen, providing open spaces that are available for locals and visitors has many other benefits apart from enhancing the beauty of the area. Aftab Majeed, an Environmental Planner with Aberdeen City Council, comments "It is recognised that open spaces play an important role in reducing and mitigating the effects of climate change and the conservation of biodiversity. They act as green lungs for the city, its residents and visitors, helping to absorb carbon emissions.

"In 2011, Aberdeen City Council published its Open Space Strategy, which sets out a

Bon Accord Terrace Gardens

new vision for the city's open spaces. With clear aims and objectives to maintain, enhance and improve the quality and accessibility of open spaces, the strategy will ensure that Aberdeen remains at the forefront of providing good quality green spaces for people to enjoy.

"Major parks in Aberdeen are maintained to a very high standard and we have two fantastic local nature conservation sites, the wildlife corridors of the River Dee and River Don. In fact, the River Dee is considered of international importance for its biodiversity, which means that it has high water quality capable of supporting species such as the Atlantic salmon, freshwater pearl mussels and otters. These areas offer great places for people to go and enjoy the scenery and the diversity of species whether it is flora or wildlife.

"Another important consideration when managing open spaces is to safeguard against the effects of climate change. For example, flooding is potentially a very important aspect of our climate changing. At Aberdeen City Council we look carefully at potential flood sites to ensure those areas have enough green spaces to help absorb surface water. Too much concrete has an adverse effect when trying to combat the effects of flash floods or water run-off. Even small areas of greenery will help to retain water.

"The Open Space Strategy that has been published recently demonstrates a strong commitment to promoting and maintaining our high quality environment and to making Aberdeen a great place for present and future generations."

Parks

Biodiversity is no more evident than at Aberdeen's most popular tourist attraction, the Winter Gardens at Duthie Park. The park, located along the banks of the River Dee on Riverside Drive, was opened to the public in 1883, from land donated by Lady Elizabeth Duthie of Ruthrieston. Within the 44 acres of the park, the Winter Gardens, at the northern end, are home to many exotic plants, including the largest collection of cacti in Britain. Rare plants from around the world are displayed within the Temperate House, Corridor of Perfumes, Fern House, Victorian Corridor, Japanese Garden, and the Tropical House and Arid House.

In contrast to the business of the Winter Gardens, with much fewer exotic species on offer, there is the more traditional Victoria Park, near the Rosemount area of the city. Named after Queen Victoria, and opened to the public in 1871, the park is home to traditional Scottish flower-beds, roses, shrubs and trees. A wonderful fountain sits in the centre of the park, made from 14 different types of granite. The fountain was presented to the citizens of the city by the Granite

Polishers and Master Builders of Aberdeen. Although located within a busy part of Aberdeen, Victoria Park is a tranquil and peaceful place to sit and enjoy the fragrances that emanate from the flora. There is a lovely 'easy access' garden for those with wheelchairs.

A little further along from Victoria Park is the spacious Westburn Park. Catering for football, tennis and grass bowling, the park is usually busy with adults and children. The Gilcomston Burn runs through the park, and modelled water features have been added to create attractions for young children. An indoor and outdoor tennis centre, which is run by the city council, provides a great venue for leisure and competitive sport.

One of the most picturesque of all parks in Aberdeen is Johnston Gardens. This small and compact park, which is surrounded by private housing in the Springfield area, is a popular place for bridal couples to get their photographs taken. The gently flowing stream that runs through the park opens into ponds that are home to mallard and Muscovy ducks. Rhododendrons, spring bulbs, heathers and alpines abound in this park, providing a very secluded setting for those seeking a gentle stroll while enjoying the sounds of nature.

If it is the unusual that is sought, there can be no better park within Aberdeen to find something 'different' than Stewart Park. Named after the Lord Provost, Sir David Stewart, the land was bought by the city council with funds bequeathed by the widow of a merchant trader in the city, John Taylor. In 1903 the captain of the Arctic whaler, *Benbow*, presented the council with two whale jawbones, which now form an arch over one of the paths in the park. Another curio in the park is the intricate fountain, designed as a replica of an Italian lavabo, sculpted by Arthur Taylor of Aberdeen.

Seaton Park lies to the north of the city. Purchased in 1947 from Major Hay, this stunning open space is popular with walkers and picnickers. At the south side the fortified towers of St Machar's Cathedral stand tall over the slopes of the park, while at the north side steep cliffs line the River Don as it meanders to the North Sea under the ancient Brig o' Balgownie.

Hazlehead Park is the largest park in Aberdeen, covering more than 400 acres. The diversity on offer is exceptional. Originally part of the Freedom Lands granted to the city in 1319, the land fell into private ownership but was bought back by the council in 1920.

Heavily wooded, Hazlehead Park is popular with walkers, naturalists and picnickers. The trails stretch for ten miles, with well-marked routes that can take up to three hours to walk. The park itself has rose gardens, a stunning collection of azaleas, rhododendrons and heather beds, and a recently renovated children's play area and pets' corner.

Hazlehead Park has a good collection of sculpture by a range of artists, including the memorial to the 167 men killed at the Piper Alpha oil disaster in 1988.

Although Hazlehead offers many attractions and a place to chill out on a warm summer's day, the park is probably more famous for the annual event that occurs on the third Sunday of June. For the past 50 years the Aberdeen Highland Games has attracted hundreds of thousands of visitors to the city. Locals and visitors enjoy watching athletes compete in the many events that test strength, endurance and skill, together with the spectacle of massed pipe bands and Highland dancers.

Highland Games

It is thought that Highland Games have their origins in the 11th century. King Malcolm III of Scotland, in an attempt to find the fastest runner to be his royal messenger, created a foot race to the summit of Craig Choinnich, a small but beautiful hill east of the village of Braemar. The ascent to the top, although short, is very steep, and would have challenged the most ardent of runners. Many historians believe that this event

sparked the start of Highland Games.

Historical records from the early 18th century suggest that members of Clan Grant were summoned to take part in a competition, wearing Highland coats and carrying "gun, sword and pistil". However, it was not until Victorian times that the modern version of the games was established. In 1832 the Braemar Highland Society donated £5 for prizes at the gathering and became the organising body for future gatherings. Queen Victoria first visited the games in 1848 and later ordered that the title Royal should be added to the name of the society. The Braemar Games are now organised by the Braemar Royal Highland Charity.

Such was the popularity of the Braemar Games, that other villages and towns in the Highlands started up their own versions. Today, there are more than 60 games held annually in Scotland, and further afield (there is a gathering in Japan), all under the auspices of the Scottish Highland Games Association. Maintaining traditions that date back 1,000 years, the association approves events for around 500 athletes to compete in front of 150,000 spectators each year.

From Aberdeen to Helensburgh, competitors gather annually to display their skills in a wide range of events. There is the famous caber toss, which involves tossing a long tapered pine pole

A piper at the Highland Games

stroll around
Hazlehead Park,
visit the animal corner
and watch nature
in action

admire the stunning
flowers of Seaton Park

trek through miles
of wooded trails in
the Hazlehead forest

visit a Highland
games meeting and
marvel at the skill and
muscle of the athletes
and grace and beauty
of the pipe bands and
dancers

Highlights

end-over-end so that the upper part of the vertical pole strikes the ground first. An athlete is said to have 'turned the caber' if the end that was held hits the ground at a 12 o'clock position measured relative to the direction of the run by the athlete.

The stone putt is similar to the event at the Olympic Games, but a large stone is used instead of the steel shot. The Braemar Stone, which weighs about 25 pounds, is propelled by the athlete from a standing position – no run-up allowed at Highland Games. Numerous other events of strength are performed at Highland Games, including the Maide Leisg (Gaelic for Lazy Stick). Two men sitting on the ground with the soles of their feet pressed against each other hold the stick between them. The objective is to pull the stick towards their bodies, thus lifting the other competitor off the ground.

Although the feats of strength are enjoyable to watch, for many people attending the games the massing of the pipe bands provides the most memorable spectacle. There can be as many as 20 pipe bands marching and playing together, resulting in a thunderous rendition of traditional Scottish favourites. Pipe competitions, including solo performances, and drumming and fiddling, are all part of the overall games' experience. Dance plays an important part of the culture of Highland

Games. Dancers from all over Scotland, and indeed from around the world, take part in various competitions. The World Championship Highland Dancing Competition is held at the Cowal Highland Gathering, at Dunoon near Glasgow.

It is not only Hazlehead Park where Highland dancing and pipe bands can be found during the summer. Right in the heart of the city centre is the three-acre Union Terrace Gardens. Once an open valley that cut through the centre of Aberdeen, the north end was closed in when a Victorian viaduct was built in 1888. Used for occasional concerts, dancing and pipe-band competitions, the gardens provide an oasis for relaxation in the city centre. Many iconic images of Aberdeen show the magnificent floral crest on the gentle slope at the north end of the gardens. The crest depicts the city's coat of arms, while at the south end there are mature elms that were planted 200 years ago.

With its many fine parks and gardens, Aberdeen really is a green city. The work of the city council ensures that diversity of species and the beauty of the natural environment can be enjoyed by those who take time to stroll around the parks and gardens. The future of Aberdeen looks rosy, perhaps allowing the city to keep up the tradition of being a top performer in the annual Britain in Bloom contest.

Highland dancing

Tropical flower in the Winter Gardens, Duthie Park

Banks of the River Dee

Exploring

Aberdeen City Council open spaces

Aberdeen has six city parks, seven local parks, 32 neighbourhood parks and many more smaller green spaces. Large parks have a number of different facilities capable of attracting crowds of residents and visitors to spend several hours or a full day. Local parks generally serve a smaller catchment area than city parks, have fewer facilities but can offer specific attractions and features.

Details of all parks in Aberdeen can be found on the Aberdeen City Council website.
www.aberdeencity.gov.uk/community_life_leisure/parks_open_spaces

Aberdeen's Open Space Strategy sets out a new vision for green spaces around the city: it aims to improve the quality of open spaces. The strategy is based on the results of a city-wide open-space audit conducted in 2010 and has been prepared with the involvement of communities, business, residents and other partner organisations. The strategy can be found on the Aberdeen City Council website.
www.aberdeencity.gov.uk/planning_environment

Hazlehead Park

Hazlehead Park is in the west end of Aberdeen, at the top of Queens Road (B9119). A short drive from the Queens Road and Kings Gate roundabout leads to a large car park. An entrance near the car park leads to the pets' corner, which contains animals such as rabbits, chinchillas, miniature donkeys, tropical fish, ducks and peacocks.

For information about the pets' corner, visit the Aberdeen City Council website.
www.aberdeencity.gov.uk/community_life_leisure/parks_open_spaces/

The spacious park offers excellent walks and picnic areas. Wooded walks can be found at the far end of the park, near to the golf course.

Continuing past the car park, the road leads to the Hazlehead Golf Club, where it is possible to play on the excellent wooded courses.

Hazlehead offers three picturesque courses and a pitch-and-putt.

Designed by Alistair McKenzie, the golf architect better known for designing the Augusta National, the Number 1 course at Hazlehead provides a true test of golf skills with gorse and woodland being the main obstacles. The second course, originally a nine-hole course, extended in the 1970s, has a more open aspect, making it suitable for those who want to brush up on their technique. The nine-hole course has wide fairways.

All courses are accessible from the main clubhouse, off Hazlehead Avenue. From the town centre, head up Queens Road on the

B9119. At the Kings Gate roundabout, take a left onto the narrow Hazlehead Avenue. Continue on this road until it ends at the clubhouse.
www.aberdeencity.gov.uk/sportaberdeen/facilities/golf

Victoria Park
Located off Westburn Road, at the junction of Westburn Drive, about two miles from the city centre, Victoria Park is one of the smallest and most beautiful parks in Aberdeen. Peace and tranquillity can be found in this green space, and there is a special garden for the disabled to enjoy.

Westburn Park
Across from Victoria Park, Westburn's spacious park caters for football and tennis and has a children's cycle track and play area.

The Westburn Tennis Centre, at the north end of the park, is a pay-and-play indoor tennis centre with no memberships. Visitors are very welcome, whether to simply knock about tennis balls for an hour, or to play a more energetic and competitive match. There are tennis coaches on hand to advise and assist. Their website has details of coaching sessions and opening times.
www.aberdeencity.gov.uk/SportAberdeen/facilities/

Duthie Park
Home to the David Welch Winter Gardens, where exotic flowers and plants can be found, Duthie Park has many features including a bandstand, fountains, ponds and statues. The park has cricket lawns, bands playing during the summer months and a boating pond with pedaloes for hire.

Duthie Park is off Riverside Drive, on the banks of the River Dee, near to the junction at Great Southern Road. A short walk over the bridge that spans the River Dee leads to another excellent open space. Although it is not a formal park, a large grass area leads to the riverbank. Walkers and picnickers enjoy this area in summer.

Johnston Gardens
Ponds, rockeries and an abundance of traditional plants and flowers make this park one of the most picturesque in the city. The gardens are on Viewfield Road, off Queens Road in the west end of Aberdeen, near to the Gordon Highlanders Museum. An exceptional day can be spent by firstly visiting the museum to view the excellent exhibitions, followed by a gentle stroll to reflect on the history of the Highlanders in the tranquillity and peace of the park.

Seaton Park
This park lies to the north of the city and was purchased by the council in 1947. Beside the park's south gates stands the historic St Machar's Cathedral. There are many fine areas in the park, including the flowerbeds, rose beds and the walled garden beside the old stables, which have been converted for housing. A whole day can be spent exploring Seaton Park, especially if a visit to the cathedral is taken in too.

Details of St Machar's Cathedral and opening times can be found on their website.
www.stmachar.com

THE GORDON HIGHLANDERS

On 15 October 2011, a new memorial to the Gordon Highlanders was unveiled in Aberdeen. Prince Charles revealed the sculpture of two soldiers at a ceremony at the Castlegate, at the top end of Union Street. The Gordon Highlanders, raised in 1794 by the Duke of Gordon, was amalgamated with the Queen's Own Highlanders in 1994 and therefore ceased to exist after that date. The sculpture is a fitting reminder of a fighting force that, with its origins embedded in Aberdeen and the surrounding north-east of Scotland, fought for king and country for 200 years.

Alexander Gordon, the 4th Duke of Gordon, raised the Gordon Highlanders in 1794. Born in Fochabers, Morayshire, and educated at Eton, Alexander Gordon was created a peer of Great Britain, as Baron Gordon of Huntly.

For the honour of defending king and country, Alexander Gordon sought permission from King George III to raise a regiment. As the king was in much need of military force, particularly because of the threat from Napoleon, permission was granted. Paying all expenses himself, the duke began recruiting around the north-east of Scotland.

"There is a very famous legend around the recruitment process of the Gordon Highlanders", comments Jesper Ericsson, curator of the Gordon Highlanders Museum in Aberdeen. "Alexander's wife, Duchess Jean, and her daughters rode around country fairs looking for suitable men for the newly formed regiment. Legend has it that men who signed up would receive not only the king's shilling but, more importantly, a kiss from the fair duchess.

"Within a few months, over 1,000 men had joined the regiment. Equipped and clothed by the duke, the men paraded for the first time in Aberdeen at the Castlegate, on 24 June 1794.

"The first Commanding Officer of The Gordon Highlanders was the Marquess of Huntly, the duke's son. He was very young, in fact, only 24 years of age."

Known officially as the 100th Regiment of Foot, since the British Army used a numerical numbering system to name its regiments, the men paraded in front of the people of Aberdeen and the day after they marched down to the docks and boarded a ship to Southampton. They spent the next four years on garrison duties in Gibraltar and Corsica. When they returned, in 1798, they were sent to fight the armies of France, first at Egmont-op-Zee in Holland in 1799, and then in Egypt, in 1801.

The regiment played a prominent role in the final defeat of Napoleon at Quatre Bras and Waterloo in 1815. Jesper Ericsson adds "At a critical point in the early afternoon of 18 June 1815, the day of Waterloo, 300 Gordons were ordered forward to counter a massive advance from 3,000 French soldiers. As they went off towards the French lines, they felt the ground rumbling and heard a sound like thunder. Turning around, they found the cavalry of the Scots Greys was fast approaching from the rear. The men from the Gordons suddenly realised that the Greys were going to ride through them and get to the French lines first! The Gordons, having none of this, grabbed onto the stirrups of the Scots Greys and held on as they approached the French. To the cry of 'Scotland forever', The Gordon Highlanders smashed into the French line and completely overpowered them."

The Afghan War
A period of peace followed and the regiment went off to places such as Ireland and India. Although the Gordon Highlanders didn't take part in the Crimean War, their soldiers did serve with other regiments fighting there. However,

it was during the Second Anglo-Afghan War of 1878–80 that the Gordon High-landers were to cement their reputation.

After tensions between Britain and Russia ended with the June 1878 Congress of Berlin, Russia turned its attention to Central Asia. Russia sent an uninvited diplomatic mission to Kabul, despite efforts by Afghan officials to keep them out. The British had always been worried about the Russians and their expanding empire encroaching onto the north-west Indian border, so when the Afghans were not quick enough to accept a British mission into the country the British decided to invade.

A British force of about 40,000 men was distributed into military columns that penetrated Afghanistan at three different points. In August 1880, a huge column of men, including the Gordon Highlanders, marched for 23 days, covering over 300 miles from Kabul to Kandahar, routing the enemy forces from the town of Kandahar and surrounding villages.

Two Gordon Highlanders won the Victoria Cross during the Second Afghan War. George Stuart White, a major in the 92nd Regiment, led an attack on a fortified hill. They came upon a body of soldiers that outnumbered his force by about eight to one. His men were exhausted from earlier battles so he

92nd storming the Asmai Heights, Afghanistan, 1897

took a rifle and went off by himself. After Major White located and shot the leader of the enemy the soldiers fled, allowing the British to take control of the vantage point.

The second VC awarded during the conflict was for 'conspicuous gallantry and bravery'. Lieutenant William Henry Dick-Cunyngham won his medal in December 1879. His citation reads "In having exposed himself to the full fire of enemy, and by his example and encouragement rallied the men who, having been beaten back, were at the moment wavering at the top of the hill". Dick-Cunyngham went on to become the

Commanding Officer of the 2nd Battalion of the Gordon Highlanders.

Amalgamation
In 1881 the Gordon Highlanders were ordered to amalgamate with one of the Lowland regiments, the 75th (Stirlingshire) Regiment of Foot. Jesper Ericsson comments "The 75th was the older regiment, they had been raised in 1787 to fight in India for the East India Company. Once raised, they left Britain and didn't return for another 20 years. Come the amalgamation there was a little uneasiness about the two regiments joining, especially from the soldiers of the 92nd. Because the 75th was the older

2nd 4th Battalion, Gordons, WW1

regiment, it was given the distinction of becoming the 1st Battalion of the Gordon Highlanders, while the original Gordon Highlanders, the 92nd, would become the 2nd Battalion.

"The men of the 1st Battalion of the Gordon Highlanders converted well to the amalgamation and were turned into good Highland soldiers. They were even taught the wearing of kilts! The 92nd brought with them the sphinx as a symbol while the 75th brought the tiger. After 1881 you will see the tiger and sphinx on belt plate badges, and the regimental journal is called Tiger and Sphinx.

"Another interesting change in uniform came during the Boer War. Camouflage came into play during this war and the Gordons had to adapt. Officers would traditionally go into battle in full uniform, wearing badges of rank and carrying swords. Kilts were uncovered and belts shone brightly. During the first battles of the war the regiment suffered heavy losses because the colours of the kilt and shine of equipment meant that men were picked off easily by the enemy. So officers were told to stop looking like officers and dress like the men."

During the First World War, the Gordon Highlanders increased rapidly in numbers. In total, 11 battalions were raised, equating to about 50,000 men. Of those, 9,000 were killed in action, with a further 20,000 wounded.

Second World War
The Second World War started badly for the Gordon Highlanders. Four battalions were sent across the Channel in late 1939 and early 1940 to serve with the British Expeditionary Force (BEF). Of those four battalions, two escaped from Dunkirk at

1815 uniform

the beginning of June 1940 and two were captured, along with the entire 51st (Highland) Division, at St Valery en Caux, almost two weeks later. In the Far East, the 2nd Battalion of the Gordon Highlanders was captured when Singapore fell on 15 February 1942. These men became prisoners of war of the Japanese and were forced to work on the 'death railway'. Jesper Ericsson reflects on the now-famous story of *The Forgotten Highlander*. "Alistair Urquhart, who became the best-selling author of his story, was a 2nd Battalion man. Coming from Aberdeen, when war broke out he went into the Gordons and served in the Far East.

He was taken prisoner but survived the camps.

"Alistair came into the museum one day, bringing his medals with him to see if they could be mounted so that he could wear them. We got our oral historian to talk with him and slowly, piece by piece, the story of his years in the prison camps emerged. His story was published in newspapers and that is when a publishing company turned his tale into a book, which went on to sell many copies. Channel Five produced a television documentary about his life."

Inside the Gordon Highlanders Museum

5th and 7th Battalion Gordons crossing the Tunisian border, 1943

Three battalions of the Gordon Highlanders took part in the Normandy landings. Soldiers from the 2nd Battalion fought in north-west Europe, from Normandy up into Holland, ending up near Hamburg in north-west Germany. Tom Duguid, veteran of the Second World War, called up in March 1943, reflects "I am very proud to have served with the 2nd Battalion of the Gordon Highlanders, although the war years were never easy.

"My first lucky escape came during our training at the Bridge of Don Barracks

in Aberdeen. We were in D Block at the barracks but we had to move out one Saturday, to make way for another squad of men. The following weekend was the big raid in Aberdeen and a bomb was dropped on D Block, killing 12 men. Luck was already on my side.

"We landed in France in June 1944, and we marched through Belgium and Holland. We had to dig slit trenches and lie flat to shield against shells. One day we were told to 'advance to contact', or in other words, move forward till fired upon. We moved into a field when all of a sudden a huge explosion occurred right in the middle of the field. Our sergeant shouted 'stand still, mines'. We stood rock solid in the field, which we later learned was riddled with anti-tank mines. Unfortunately one of our platoon was killed when the mine detonated. Engineers came and marked a safe route for us to walk over to escape from the field.

"Our platoon advanced towards the River Rhine during wintertime of 1944. Thankfully, we were out of the front line for Christmas and the officers served our dinner. However, during our meal a shell came down just outside the building we had occupied. The first thing we did was to shield our Christmas meal with our arms and hands, so that plaster dust didn't spoil our food. But we went back to the fighting line for Hogmanay.

"We crossed the Rhine in the spring of 1945. Our division got the nickname the 'river crossers' because we crossed and captured several key crossing points including one on the Seine, the Rhine and then the Elbe. We ended up near Hamburg in north-west Germany, securing key crossings and roads as we went nearer to the heart of the country."

Gordon Highlanders were known for their ability to fight on foot. But they were also well known for their flexibility.

Jesper Ericsson reflects "Soldiers from the regiment fought in Burma in 1944 and 1945. Sailing by boat to India, fully expecting to fight as infantry, they were told on their arrival in the Far East about their new role – driving tanks and using anti-tank guns! Initially they were given American Grant tanks but these were later replaced with Shermans. So up to this point their whole history had been that of infantry but then these Gordons found themselves in a completely different role. Actually, there is another little piece of military history here because 116th Regiment (Gordon Highlanders) Royal Armoured Corps was the last tank unit to be withdrawn from frontline service in the Second World War.

"Here at the Gordon Highlanders Museum we are blessed to have Second World War veterans as our volunteers. We have one who was only 18 years old when he took part in D-Day and we have another who fought at El Alamein in October 1942.

The veterans, together with the other 180 volunteers, staff the museum daily, so there are always people on hand to talk to visitors and school children. There is nothing better than having a veteran taking someone on a tour of the museum, telling you about the history and reflecting on their experiences of the war."

visit the museum to learn
about the history of a brave
and loyal regiment

examine the unique
collection of weapons
in the armory

enjoy a cake and a drink in the museum tearoom, which overlooks a wonderful and picturesque garden

reflect on the achievements of a great fighting force at the commemorative monument at the Castlegate

Highlights

HRH Prince Charles

After the Second World War the regiment took part in peacekeeping and anti-terrorist operations in Malaya, Borneo, Cyprus, Germany and Northern Ireland, with detachments serving in the Gulf Wars and in Bosnia.

End of an era

In 1994, 200 years of proud history and service came to an end when the Gordon Highlanders was ordered to amalgamate with the Queen's Own Highlanders to form 1st Battalion The Highlanders. Jesper Ericsson adds, "1st Battalion The

Highlanders existed for exactly 12 years until March 2006 when the new Royal Regiment of Scotland was created. Actually, the 1st Battalion was on tour in Iraq on that day so they formed up on parade in Basra and took off their 1st Battalion badges and put on their Royal Regiment of Scotland badges. They are now known as The Highlanders 4th Battalion The Royal Regiment of Scotland, or 4SCOTS for short.

"Although the Gordon Highlanders ceased to exist after 1994 the 4SCOTS carry the

Gordons' history with them. Our museum in Aberdeen is a living memory to the traditions and history of the regiment and, as long as The Highlanders exist, or whatever future unit they become, our museum will continue to tell their story.

"The Gordon Highlanders Museum is the only institution in the world that is dedicated to preserving the legacy and the heritage of the regiment and we are located in a splendid building in the west end of Aberdeen.

"The building that is home to the museum was bought in 1960 for use as the regimental headquarters. It was a place for officers to work and for retired officers to come and relax. Once owned by Sir George Reid, a famous Aberdeen artist who worked in the late 19th century, the building changed hands when the Ministry of Defence purchased it. It is interesting because Sir George was once a member of a militia battalion that eventually became a battalion of the Gordon Highlanders. Although he was never a Gordon I think he would be proud that his property became the museum.

"When the Gordon Highlanders ceased to exist in 1994 there was a massive 'Save the Gordons' campaign in Aberdeen. Led by Lieutenant-General Sir Peter Graham, who had a very distinguished military career, the fundraising efforts to pay for

the museum were remarkable. The local population fully supported the idea of a museum and large sums of money were raised.

"In 1997 the Gordon Highlanders Museum opened to the public. We get about 40,000 people visiting the museum every year. We recently did an exhibition about prisoners-of-war and lots of local families came forward with stories about their relatives. We are one of only two five-star museums in Aberdeen and we are very proud of that, and of the legacy from such a wonderful and brave group of first-class soldiers."

From the raising of the Gordon Highlanders in 1794, to the numerous men who have been awarded the Victoria Cross in recognition of their bravery for king, queen and country, the legacy of the Gordons has been preserved thanks to the dedicated staff at the museum.

Whether it be to learn a little more about the regiment, the war years, or simply to enjoy the excellent museum and exhibits, a visit to the Gordon Highlanders Museum in Aberdeen is most definitely an essential 'thing to do'.

Exploring

The Gordon Highlanders Museum

The Gordon Highlanders is one of the great names in Scottish history and one of the most celebrated regiments of the British Army. Renowned as a courageous fighting force with an exceptional reputation for good conduct, professionalism and steadfastness, their legacy lives on through the current-serving soldiers and through the work of the museum in Aberdeen.

The museum is home to the regimental treasures of the Gordons. The collections comprise uniforms, silver, weapons, textiles, art and a vast archive of papers, diaries and documents as well as over 4,000 medals including 11 Victoria Crosses. These items relate to the unique 200-year history.

The Armoury

Step into the armoury and come face-to-face with an impressive display of British Army swords, bayonets, knives, rifles and fire-arms, together with many allied and enemy weapons.

The Grant Room

The main gallery space allows the visitor to relive the Gordons' dramatic 200-year history, from the Napoleonic War to modern-day conflict. Real-life experiences are at the heart of the Grant Room and there are interactive stations, original film footage and life-sized reproductions to be enjoyed.

Within the Grant Room the exhibition space has been carefully laid out. Exhibits are exceptionally well preserved and information sheets are there to help tell their story, like the one about the drummer who won his Victoria Cross:

During the First Battle of Ypres in October 1914, Drummer Kenny of the 2nd Battalion Gordon Highlanders repeatedly went out under enemy fire to rescue wounded men. He had also twice retrieved one of the Battalion's machine-guns and carried messages, all the while under heavy fire.

The 2nd Battalion had been in Egypt when war broke out and had only just arrived in Belgium, where German forces were trying to strike at the Channel ports. The defensive fighting around Ypres just managed to stop the German advance.

The 1st Battalion had been in action earlier but had been forced to surrender after being cut off during the British retreat from Mons.

As a drummer, Kenny's job in action would have been as a 'runner', taking messages between different parts of the Battalion. This role echoed earlier times when drummers used to send signals by beat of drum. Drummer Kenny was a veteran of the Boer War. In addition to the Victoria Cross, he also received the Cross of St George for gallantry from Russia, Britain's wartime ally.

Courage and dedication to duty are synonymous with soldiers from the Gordon Highlanders, as one of the exhibits confirms:

During the attack at Magersfontein in December 1899, while under heavy fire, Captain Towse attempted to carry his mortally wounded Commanding Officer to safety. Four months later, at Mount Thaba, he showed great bravery again while securing an isolated position against an overwhelming Boer attack.

While the 2nd Battalion of the Gordons was under siege in Ladysmith, the 1st Battalion arrived in South Africa. It first saw action in the disastrous Battle of Magersfontein, when the Highland Brigade suffered extremely heavy losses at the hands of well-dug-in Boer marksmen. Although Gordons' casualties were comparatively light, the Battalion lost its Commanding Officer, despite the efforts of Towse and others to bring him to safety.

During the second action in April 1900, Towse was badly wounded and blinded in both eyes. Although this ended his military career, Towse worked hard to overcome his disability, devoting the rest of his life to working for the blind. In the First World War, he worked in the military hospitals in France writing letters to the families of the badly wounded.

Family History

There is an extensive archive relating to the history of the regiment. War diaries, letters, poems, scrapbooks and photograph albums are among the rich store of primary material that is available to the public. A team of experienced volunteer researchers is on hand to help with enquiries and there is an enquiry section on their website for people to submit their research queries.

Location

The Gordon Highlanders Museum is located on Viewfield Road. From the city centre the best route is to travel along Albyn Place and then Queens Road. Viewfield Road is second on the left after crossing the Anderson Drive roundabout.

www.gordonhighlanders.com

15 things to do...
...to explore
Aberdeen

Information in this book was correct at the time of publication.
For updated information please visit www.15thingstodo.com

If you have explored some of the 'things to do' that are mentioned
in this book please take a few moments to write a comment on
the website.

www.15thingstodo.com

Keep a lookout for great photographic and writing competitions
on the website and watch out for other books in the 15 things
to do series.

Coming soon

15 things to do....to explore Scotland
15 things to do....to explore the Great Glen
15 things to do....to explore Royal Deeside
15 things to do....to explore the Isle of Skye